COMPREHENSIVE RESEARCH
AND STUDY GUIDE

Poets of
World War I

Rupert Brooke
&
Siegfried Sassoon

BLOOM'S
MAJOR POETS

Maya Angelou
Elizabeth Bishop
William Blake
Gwendolyn Brooks
Robert Browning
Geoffrey Chaucer
Samuel Taylor Coleridge
Hart Crane
E. E. Cummings
Dante
Emily Dickinson
John Donne
H. D.
T. S. Eliot
Robert Frost
Seamus Heaney
Homer
A. E. Housman
Langston Hughes
John Keats
John Milton
Sylvia Plath
Edgar Allan Poe
Poets of World War I
Shakespeare's Poems & Sonnets
Percy Shelley
Wallace Stevens
Mark Strand
Alfred, Lord Tennyson
Walt Whitman
William Carlos Williams
William Wordsworth
William Butler Yeats

Poets of World War I

Rupert Brooke

&

Siegfried Sassoon

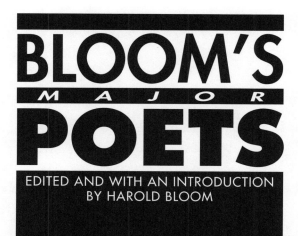

First Printing
1 3 5 7 9 8 6 4 2

Library of Congress Cataloging-in-Publication Data

Poets of World War I : Rupert Brooke and Siegfried Sassoon / edited and
with an introduction by Harold Bloom.
    p. cm. — (Bloom's major poets)
Includes bibliographical references and index.
    ISBN 0-7910-7388-2
    1. Brooke, Rupert, 1887-1915—Criticism and interpretation. 2.
Sassoon, Siegfried, 1886-1967—Criticism and interpretation. 3. World
War, 1914-1918—Great Britain—Literature and the war. 4. Soldiers'
writings, English—History and criticism. 5. War poetry, English—
History and criticism. I. Bloom, Harold. II. Series.
    PR6003.R4Z7235 2003
    821'.91209358—dc21

                                            2003006927

Chelsea House Publishers
1974 Sproul Road, Suite 400
Broomall, PA 19008-0914

www.chelseahouse.com

Contributing Editor: Kate Cambor

Produced by: www.book*designing*.com

Contents

User's Guide

This volume is designed to present biographical, critical, and bibliographical information on the author's best-known or most important poems. Following Harold Bloom's editor's note and introduction is a detailed biography of the author, discussing major life events and important literary accomplishments. A thematic and structural analysis of each poem follows, tracing significant themes, patterns, and motifs in the work.

A selection of critical extracts, derived from previously published material from leading critics, analyzes aspects of each poem. The extracts consist of statements from the author, if available, early reviews of the work, and later evaluations up to the present. A bibliography of the author's writings (including a complete list of all books written, cowritten, edited, and translated), a list of additional books and articles on the author and the work, and an index of themes and ideas in the author's writings conclude the volume.

~

Harold Bloom is Sterling Professor of the Humanities at Yale University and Henry W. and Albert A. Berg Professor of English at the New York University Graduate School. He is the author of over 20 books, including *Shelley's Mythmaking* (1959), *The Visionary Company* (1961), *Blake's Apocalypse* (1963), *Yeats* (1970), *A Map of Misreading* (1975), *Kabbalah and Criticism* (1975), *Agon: Toward a Theory of Revisionism* (1982), *The American Religion* (1992), *The Western Canon* (1994), and *Omens of Millennium: The Gnosis of Angels, Dreams, and Resurrection* (1996). *The Anxiety of Influence* (1973) sets forth Professor Bloom's provocative theory of the literary relationships between the great writers and their predecessors. His most recent books include *Shakespeare: The Invention of the Human*, a 1998 National Book Award finalist, and *How to Read and Why*, which was published in 2000.

Professor Bloom earned his Ph.D. from Yale University in 1955 and has served on the Yale faculty since then. He is a 1985 MacArthur Foundation Award recipient, served as the Charles Eliot Norton Professor of Poetry at Harvard University in 1987–88, and has received honorary degrees from the universities of Rome and Bologna. In 1999, Professor Bloom received the prestigious American Academy of Arts and Letters Gold Medal for Criticism.

Currently, Harold Bloom is the editor of numerous Chelsea House volumes of literary criticism, including the series BLOOM'S NOTES, BLOOM'S MAJOR DRAMATISTS, BLOOM'S MAJOR NOVELISTS, MAJOR LITERARY CHARACTERS, MODERN CRITICAL VIEWS, MODERN CRITICAL INTERPRETATIONS, and WOMEN WRITERS OF ENGLISH AND THEIR WORKS.

Editor's Note

My Introduction, accepting the poetic limitations of Rupert Brooke and Siegfried Sassoon in comparison to the greatness of Wilfred Owen and Isaac Rosenberg, still tries to isolate what remains of value in these two lesser poets of World War I.

Sassoon's best critic remains John Middleton Murry, who catches the precise accent of the Hindenberg Line poems. But all the other exegetes of Sassoon's war poems who are excerpted here, impress me as being wholly adequate to their subject.

The unique personality and lasting spell of Rupert Brooke are recaptured by Virginia Woolf, Winston Churchill, and Henry James.

Introduction

HAROLD BLOOM

1.

Rupert Brooke can be termed rather more a personal legend than a literary one. His handsomeness, social charm, and somewhat Byronic sexual ambiguity fascinated his friends Henry James and Virginia Woolf, and his English patriotism inspired Winston Churchill. As a poet, he owes much to Swinburne, and his disciples, Oscar Wilde and Ernest Dowson. His best work is not the famous "1914" sequence of five sonnets, but the Swinburnian "The Song of the Beasts," the very Georgian "The Old Vicarage, Grantchester," and "The Great Lover," a reflection of a peaceful sojourn in Tahiti.

Of the war poems, the best is probably "The Soldier," which survives its English self-satisfaction mostly because of its abnegation in attempting to dismiss Brooke's own self:

> If I should die, think only this of me:
>   That there's some corner of a foreign field
> That is for ever England. There shall be
>   In that rich earth a richer dust concealed;
> A dust whom England bore, shaped, made aware,
>   Gave, once, her flowers to love, her ways to roam,
> A body of England's, breathing English air,
>   Washed by the rivers, blest by suns of home.
>
> And think, this heart, all evil shed away,
>   A pulse in the eternal mind, no less
>   Gives somewhere back the thoughts by England given;
> Her sights and sounds; dreams happy as her day;
>   And laughter, learnt of friends; and gentleness,
>   In hearts at peace, under an English heaven.

It is too easy to dismiss this now as mere smugness, as many critics have done. Doubtless E. M. Forster and Henry James were attracted by Brooke's repressed homosexuality, and his beauty, but they and Virginia Woolf all were remarkable readers. Brooke's gifts as a poet were palpable, but it has been his sad fate to be obscured by the major poetry of Wilfred Owen and Isaac Rosenberg.

2.

Siegfried Sassoon, talented and prolific in both verse and prose, survives now only as an effective anti-war poet, though he has nothing of his friend Wilfred Owen's power or of Isaac Rosenberg's uncanny originality. The best of his poems seems to me "The Rear-Guard," with its superb ending:

> Alone he staggered on until he found
> Dawn's ghost that filtered down a shafted stair
> To the dazed, muttering creatures underground
> Who hear the boom of shells in muffled sound.
> At last with sweat of horror in his hair,
> He climbed through darkness to the twilight air
> Unloading hell behind him step by step.

There is a directness and vividness in Sassoon's poems of the Hindenburg Line in 1917, that he never matched again. There is however lasting eloquence and prophetic warning in "Aftermath," written in March 1919, with its famous close:

> *Have you forgotten yet? . . .*
> *Look up, and swear by the green of the spring that you'll never forget.* ❀

Biography of
Rupert Brooke

Rupert Brooke in many ways embodies the legends about the Great War that were subsequently made famous by historians and literary scholars like Robert Wohl, Paul Fussel, and Mondris Eksteins. Handsome, charming, and talented, Brooke was a national hero even before his death at the age of 27 in 1915. His poetry, brimming with patriotism and a graceful lyricism, reflected the hopes and beliefs of a country that had yet to feel the full, devastating effects of the war. His early death only solidified his image as "a golden-haired, blue-eyed English Adonis."

Brooke's early years were typical of a well-to-do childhood. He attended a prestigious boarding school—Rugby, where his father was a headmaster—studied Latin and Greek, and began to write poetry. He expressed an early enthusiasm for the English Decadent poets of the 1890s (Wilde, Dowson, and Swinburne) before turning to Baudelaire and the French Symbolists.

His family took for granted that Brooke would go on to one of the great English universities, and in 1906 he entered Cambridge. During his three years there, Brooke quickly established himself in English intellectual circles, counting among his acquaintances Virginia Woolf, writer Lytton Strachey, economist John Maynard Keynes and his brother Geoffrey (later to become Brooke's bibliographer), and the poet William Butler Yeats. Although his poetry from this time is generally considered of little significance, aided by his charm and good looks, he became an increasingly conspicuous literary figure.

From the time of his graduation in 1909 to the start of World War I in 1914, Brooke spent most of his time writing and traveling. His poetry during this period, which still emphasized the themes of love and nature, resembled that of most of the poets of his generation, including D. H. Lawrence, John Drinkwater, and Walter de la Mare. One of his most popular poems was published during this era in *Georgian Poetry*. It is titled "The Old Vicarage, Grantchester," after a small village near Cambridge where Brooke lived for a time after 1909.

Mid-1912 was one of the most turbulent periods in Brooke's life. Confused by homosexual impulses and frustrated by the rejection of a woman with whom he was in love, his sexual crisis culminated in a nervous breakdown. Brooke spent several months in rehabilitation, during which period he was not allowed to write poetry. By summer, though, he had recovered enough to travel to Germany, a trip that marked the beginning of almost three years of constant travel.

In May of 1913, he went to the United States, where he spent four months before sailing to the South Pacific. Three of the seven months he remained in the Pacific were spent in Tahiti, where he wrote some of his best poems, including "Tiare Tahiti" and "The Great Lover." He found considerable happiness during this era of his life.

In the spring of 1914, Brooke decided to return to England. Within a few months of his return, World War I began, and like most men of his social station, Brooke quickly volunteered for service. He joined the Royal Navy Volunteer Reserve, whose first destination was Antwerp, Belgium, where it stayed through the beginning of 1915. The Reserve saw little fighting during this time, and it was a productive period for Brooke. He produced his best-known poetry, the group of five war sonnets titled "1914."

These sonnets were immediately famous. On Easter Sunday in 1915, the dean of St. Paul's Cathedral in London, William Ralph Inge, read aloud "The Soldier." Brooke's death three weeks later insured that his name would always be intertwined with the war sonnets, and with "The Soldier" in particular.

In February of 1915, Brooke was ordered to sail to the Dardanelles—a strait between Europe and Turkey—for the Gallipoli campaign that would begin that spring. During the journey, however, Brooke contracted blood poisoning. He died on April 23 on a ship in the Aegean Sea and was buried in an olive grove on the Greek island of Skyros. Grief over Brooke's death was felt throughout his country. Many during this early stage of the war believed him to represent the ideal of patriotic and noble sacrifice.

After the staggering number of deaths that the English incurred during the trench warfare of 1916 and 1917, however, such patriotic feeling—like Brooke's poetry—came to be seen as naïve. A more realistic poetry emerged out of the shock of the trenches, replacing

Brooke's poetry as the most important literary expression of the war. Poets such as Wilfred Owen, Siegfried Sassoon, and Isaac Rosenberg captured the terror and tragedy of modern warfare; next to their poetry, Brooke's war sonnets seemed highly romantic and unrealistic.

Since his death, Brooke's poetry, while always popular, has been often dismissed by critics charging that Brooke's "mind remained to the end that of a clever public schoolboy" and that his poetry had "no inside." One critic, Julian Tennyson, writing in 1943, complained that Brooke's war sonnets were "beautiful, perhaps, but nonetheless a little silly, even school-girlish." These charges implying the "adolescence" of Brooke's prewar verse reflect the new social consciousness and pessimism that poetry assumed in the 1920s, after the publication of T. S. Eliot's *The Waste Land*.

By contrast, the "effete pastoralism" that characterized much Georgian poetry represented an attempt to escape from the realities of modern urban industrial life. Despite such extreme and varying opinions, however, most critics agree that Brooke's poetry remains important as a reflection of the pre-war mood in England. ❀

Thematic Analysis of
"1914: I. Peace"

"Peace" has long been one of the most popular of Rupert Brooke's *1914* sonnets. Like much of Brooke's poetry, "Peace" reveals Brooke's rather romantic—some might even say sentimental—vision of the war, a vision unencumbered by much actual experience. The poem celebrates the discovery of a cause and the eager anticipation of the regeneration of "a world grown old and cold and weary." Like the other poems in *1914*, "Peace" is a poem of mythic power, with Brooke as the archetypal Apollo in the sacrificial role of hero-as-victim.

Later poets would often contrast an idyllic and longed-for pre-war life with the misery and brutality of life among the trenches, highlighting the destruction of a once good and rational world. Brooke, however, here maintains the attitude that the war would purify and cleanse a corrupted and sickly population.

Brooke first identifies the impending war as part of God's grand design. Those who respond to His calling will "leave the sick hearts that honour could not move, / And half-men, and their dirty songs and dreary, / And all the little emptiness of love!" Excluding any reference to the war itself while he renders the grim realities of the war bland and even irrelevant, Brooke presents the reader with an abstract vision of warfare. He thereby offers the promise of a mythic regeneration and general revitalization.

Brooke, the poet *and* soldier, is himself prayerfully thankful for the moral challenge afforded by the war, a challenge seen not in terms of an outward wrong to be righted but in terms of an opportunity for personal moral rebirth. This position gives the views expressed in "Peace" more credence. They are at once beautiful, noble, and transcendent; supposedly, these sentiments are available to any combatant.

In the sestet, Brooke continues to build his image of a world emptied of the limitations of physical deprivation and mortal danger. "Oh! We, who have known shame, we have found release there, / Where there's no ill, no grief, but sleep has mending." Psychologically, this formulation offers the possibility of feeling morally pure despite physical degradation. The poem thus ends with a comforting paradox: for the volunteer, the sufferings of warfare bring a spiritual "peace," for in battle "the worst friend and enemy is but Death."

The peace referred to in the title could be interpreted in one of two ways—either as a reference to the long years of peace before 1914 or to the "laughing heart's long peace," which the war is said to have brought about. Brooke may also have been referring to his passionate and at times unhappy amorous entanglements with Ka Cox and Cathleen Nesbitt—or to his emotional involvement with Lytton Strachey and other male members of the Bloomsbury circle.

Brooke's subsequent nervous breakdown and "wandering" caused him to reevaluate his former friends. He turned his back on feminism, Bloomsbury, and much else that he perceived as "modern." As he wrote to a friend, "Please don't breathe a word of it. I want to keep such shreds of reputation as I have left. Yet it's true. For I sit and stare at the thing and have the purest Nineteenth Century grandiose thoughts, about the Destiny of Man, the Irreversibility of Fate, the Doom of Nations, the fact that Death awaits us All, and so forth. Wordsworth Revidivus. Oh dear! oh dear!"

The war offered Brooke the chance to escape a sexually confused past and the threat of middle-age monotony that lay before him. It would be the "release" he speaks of in "Peace."

But while John Lehmann acknowledges that the poem might have struck a chord with readers anxiously attending the beginning of hostilities in the early months of the war, he insists that "looked at dispassionately today, it is difficult not to feel that it is riddled with sentimentality and narcissistic fantasy." Moreover, he demands, "What soldier, who had experienced the meaningless horror and foulness of the Western Front stalemate in 1916 and 1917, could think of it as a place to greet 'as swimmers into cleanness leaping' or as a welcome relief 'from a world grown old and cold and weary'?"

A contemporary of Brooke, fellow poet Charles Sorley, also objected to the poem on similar grounds. "He is far too obsessed with his own sacrifice, regarding the going to war of himself (and others) as a highly intense, remarkable and sacrificial exploit, whereas it is merely the conduct demanded of him (and others) by the turn of circumstances. . . . He has clothed his attitude in fine words: but he has taken the sentimental attitude." ❁

Critical Views on
"1914: I. Peace"

TIMOTHY ROGERS ON THE ORIGINS OF THE
1914 SONNETS

[Timothy Rogers is the author of *Rupert Brooke: A Reappraisal and Selection from His Writings, Some Hitherto Unpublished* (1971) and *Georgian Poetry: 1911–1922* (1977), as well as a frequent contributor to the *Times Literary Supplement*. In this selection, Rogers situates the War Sonnets within the context of the hopeful and romantic public attitudes about the war in the early years of the conflict.]

The first tentative jottings of four of the '1914' sonnets were made in a small field-notebook. Interspersed among them are notes from military lectures—"Every officer should be easily found,' 'German explosive shells carry further back than forward,' 'Keep *strict* discipline'—and personal memoranda— 'Thompson, Officers' Mess, doesn't make his bed up,' 'Wanted: 1 curtain . . . table . . . chairs.' It is well that the beginnings of these idealistic sonnets should be thus preserved among tokens of a more practical concern. At the same time they are poems, not of war, but of preparation for war (Brooke's first title for 'The Soldier' was 'The Recruit'). The attitude to war expressed in them recalls Lord Reading's picture of him in August 1914 at a parade in Regent's Park:

> . . . clad in civilian clothes but equipped with rifle
> and haversack, and he had crowned this hybrid 'turnout'
> with a rakish, challenging, wide-brimmed black felt
> hat, worn with the air of an ancient Greek turned
> modern Mexican, which was the Poet's latest gesture
> of freedom before capitulating to the uniform drab.

The late Professor J. B. Trend suggested that contemporary leaders in *The Morning Post* might have prompted Brooke's attitude in the sonnets and been the source of some of the expressions in them. We may not accept this suggestion as it stands; Brooke was always capable of thinking for himself, nor at the height of his enthusiasm would he have succumbed to and reiterated the naïve sentiments expressed in that newspaper. But the articles do show that many of his ideas were 'in the air' at the time. Expressions that 'manly animosities of war' are preferable to the sloth, selfishness and cowardice of a 'a shameful peace' ('. . . war is not altogether an evil: it cleans and purifies: it invigorates . . .'), that 'the soul of England is the soul of the sum of Englishmen living and dead,' and that all people are 'parts of a great whole, whose destiny and interest are of infinitely higher importance than their own'—all these are exactly reflected in the sonnets.

They are reflected, too, in the writings of other poets at this time, in none more than in the jubilant John Freeman's:

> A common beating is in the air—
> The heart of England throbbing everywhere.
> And all her roads are nerves of noble thought,
> And all her people's brain is but her brain;
> Now all her history
> Is part of her requickened consciousness—
> Her courage rises clean again.

It is well to remember, too, that the feelings of those two poets who, more vividly than any, were to express the later mood of disillusion, were very different in the early months. Wilfred Owen at the outset felt a sense of 'new crusade and modern knightliness.' In the summer of 1915, shortly after Brooke's death, Siegfried Sassoon could write in 'Absolution':

> The anguish of the earth absolves our eyes
> Till beauty shines in all that we can see.
> War is our scourge; yet war has made us wise,
> And, fighting for our freedom, we are free.
>
> Horror of wounds and anger at the foe,
> And loss of things desired; all these must pass.
> We are the happy legion, for we know
> Time's but a golden wind that shakes the grass.

> —Timothy Rogers, *Rupert Brooke: A Reappraisal and Selection from His Writings, Some Hitherto Unpublished* (London: Routledge and Kegan Paul, 1971): pp. 8–9.

John Lehmann on Brooke's Puritanism

[John Lehmann was a writer and editor associated with Leonard and Virginia Woolf's Hogarth Press; he is credited with helping launch the careers of such well-known writers as W. H. Auden, Saul Bellow, and Gore Vidal. His works include *Virginia Woolf and Her World* (1975), *Thrown to the Woolfs: Leonard and Virginia Woolf and the Hogarth Press* (1978), *Rupert Brooke: His Life and His Legend* (1980), *Poets of the First World War* (1982), and *In My Own Time: Memoirs of a Literary Life*. In this excerpt from *Rupert Brooke: His Life and His Legend,* Lehmann criticizes "Peace" for displaying Brooke's peculiar brand of Puritanism, which, he suggests, emerged in reaction to the poet's earlier romantic entanglements within the Bloomsbury group.]

The two most quoted and probably most popular sonnets— certainly most popular at the time—are the first, *Peace,* and the fifth, *The Soldier.* The first, *Peace,* is the sonnet that most successors of a younger generation, and probably most soldiers who saw more of the war than Rupert ever saw, have jibbed at as shallowy sentimental and unrealistic. What soldier, who had experienced the meaningless horror and foulness of the Western Front stalemate in 1916 and 1917, could think of it as a place to greet 'as swimmers into cleanness leaping' or as a welcome relief 'from a world grown old and cold and weary'? These are the sentiments of one who at least had had no opportunity to face the reality of twentieth-century warfare—killing and maiming and being killed and maimed in the most appalling ways by the most devilish devices of terror. To say that is not to deny admiration for those, in both wars, who were aware of what they were facing and chose it out of determination to defend what they believed was worth defending— and Rupert Brooke might well have been one of those if he had lived and been active as a soldier in 1917; nor to deny that such an attitude as finds expression in *Peace* was common to many poets, on both sides of the frontiers, in the curious excitement and hysteria that the outbreak of war in 1914 aroused.

What is peculiarly disturbing about *Peace* is that it gives sudden and violent expression to Rupert's always latent puritanism. The soldiers are awakened 'from sleeping' and are leaping 'into cleanness' in getting away from their everyday pursuits (though *The Dead* seems to express an entirely opposite point of view); fighting redeems a world 'grown old and cold and weary' even though it involves killing and destruction and waste; the whole of Rupert's past life is characterized as

> The sick hearts that honour could not move,
> And half-men, and their dirty songs and dreary,
> And all the little emptiness of love.

Who are these 'half-men' and 'sick hearts' unmoved by honour? What poet was singing 'dirty songs and dreary'? Were his passionate and unhappy involvements with Ka Cox and his new, joyful love for Cathleen Nesbitt to be brushed aside as 'all the little emptiness of love'? Or was he thinking again, obsessively, of the emotional shocks he endured at Lulworth in the New Year of 1912, with Lytton Strachey and other denizens of Bloomsbury as the 'sick hearts' and 'half-men' who wounded him so mysteriously? And if so, why did they now become symbols of all that had made up civilian existence before the war, as if civilized peaceful living itself was only worth throwing away *in toto*?

—John Lehmann, *Rupert Brooke: His Life and His Legend* (London: Weidenfeld and Nicolson, 1980): pp. 136–37.

BERNARD BERGONZI ON THE MYTH OF RUPERT BROOKE

[Bernard Bergonzi is a writer whose works include *Descartes and the Animals: Poems 1948–54* (1954), *The Early H. G. Wells: A Study of the Scientific Romances* (1961), *Heroes' Twilight: A Study of the Literature of the Great War* (1965), and *Gerard Manley Hopkins* (1977). In this selection from *Heroes' Twilight,* Bergonzi discusses the origins of the myth of Rupert Brooke.]

Yet of all the myths which dominated the English consciousness during the Great War the greatest, and the most enduring, is that which enshrines the name and memory of Rupert Brooke: in which three separate elements—Brooke's personality, his death, and his poetry (or some of it)—are fused into a single image. Brooke was the first of the 'war poets'; a quintessential young Englishman; one of the fairest of the nation's sons; a ritual sacrifice offered as evidence of the justice of the cause for which England fought. His sonnet, 'The Soldier,' is among the most famous short poems in the language. If the Tolstoyan theory of art had any validity it would be one of the greatest—as, indeed, it is considered to be by the numerous readers for whom the excellence of poetry lies in the acceptability of its sentiments rather than in the quality of its language.

Brooke's personal legend was first embodied in Frances Cornford's epigram, written whilst he was still an undergraduate:

> A young Apollo, golden-haired,
> Stands dreaming on the verge of strife,
> Magnificently unprepared
> For the long littleness of life.

This already contains the essentials of the myth which was to develop during Brooke's life and then to burgeon luxuriantly after his death in April 1915. Already, during the poet's life, it seems to have been self-perpetuating: the image of the 'young Apollo, golden-haired' was given physical reality in the rather deplorable photograph taken by Sherril Schell in 1913, showing Brooke with bare shoulders and flowing locks, which formed the frontispiece of *1914 and other poems* (1915). Christopher Hassall records that this photograph was not well received by Brooke's friends, who referred to it as 'Your Favourite Actress'; one of them suggested that he might as well be photographed completely in the nude. The extravagances in the legend were played down in Edward Marsh's posthumous memoir, which fixed the public image of the dead poet: handsome, talented, theatrical, with a rather frenetic gaiety; a product of the Cambridge milieu which when transported to London produced the Bloomsbury ethos: Brooke disliked its upholders but shared many of its ideals—the cult of personal relations, in particular. There was also Brooke's social idealism which made him an enthusiastic Fabian, and the hints, scattered through many of his poems, of an energetic but rather soulful amorist. In Christopher Hassall's massive biography we are now told as much as we can conveniently assimilate about Brooke's short and favoured life. Hassall fills in the picture about aspects of Brooke's personality which Marsh left in tactful silence. It's interesting to know, for instance, that Brooke was psychologically unstable, with a paranoid streak, and for quite long periods was on the edge of a nervous breakdown: for several years he was involved in a singularly gruelling love affair that brought him little happiness. As his life becomes part of history, Brooke's legend, one may assume, will lose some of its former glamour; Hassall's book, by its sheer density of detail, may well hasten the process of demythologization. But Brooke's life will continue to be interesting, and will never lack some kind of archetypal quality, if only because he was such a perfect symbol of the doomed aspirations of Liberal England: a figure from an unwritten, or suppressed, novel by his friend, E. M. Forster.

—Bernard Bergonzi, Heroes' Twilight: A Study of the Literature of the Great War (London: Constable and Company, 1965): pp. 36–37.

Thematic Analysis of
"1914: III. The Dead" and
"1914: IV. The Dead"

The third and fourth sonnets in the 1914 series were begun as, one after another, reports came of Brooke's school friends, killed or missing. "The Dead" (I) may have used the theme found in W. E. Henley's "The Last Post," which began "Blow, you bugles of England, blow." In Brooke's eyes, Henley stood for what was best in imperialism, and while at Rubgy, Brooke had written of Henley, "One may hate, as I do, the way in which he loved England, but one cannot deny the sincerity of his love and the power of his expression of it." Brooke himself was not overwhelmingly pleased with his five war sonnets. He wrote on March 21, 1915, to his friend Sybil Pye: "Did you like them? I'm glad. I thought 4 and 5 good: the rest poor, but not worthless."

In "The Dead" (I), Brooke continues to preach his message of the transforming power of death in battle. The ultimate sacrifice required by one's country—pouring out "the red / Sweet wine of youth"—leads to immortality. The poem's octet is a list of the treasures, "rarer gifts than gold," that the dead bequeath to their survivors: years "Of work and joy," the possibility of living until a serene old age, and "those who would not have been," that is, their sons. Brooke himself had begun to regret what he considered a misspent youth; in particular, he regretted not having any children.

In the sestet of "The Dead" (I), Brooke presents those human qualities that we only discover through the sacrifice of the dead, qualities he felt his own life somehow lacked. "Holiness," "Love," "Pain," "Honour," "Nobleness"—these are the elements of that lauded heritage he was missing. That these ideals are linked in Brooke's mind to kingly attributes only furthers the gulf he sees between those who continue to live past their youth and those who give up their lives and die a glorious death.

The theme of patrimony is an important one in "The Dead" (I). As Robert Wohl observes in his book, *The Generation of 1914*, "The war had arrived unexpectedly, like a legacy from an unknown relative, to save Brooke from a fate he had long feared. It provided an escape from the dreary sleep of middle age and conventional living." Even if he had occasionally seen the declaration of war as an awkward interruption of his usual life, by the time he wrote these poems, the war experience linked him to an older and more pure tradition and way of living.

In "The Dead" (II), the fourth sonnet in the *1914 Sonnets,* Brooke continues his meditation on the glorious immortality bestowed on youth by their patriotic sacrifice. Adopting the octet-sestet form of most of the other poems in this series, "The Dead" (II) begins with an overview of human experience as it is lived through the senses and emotions. Through both the joys and sorrows, this life has a certain "kindness," associated with the gentle rays of the sun ("Dawn was theirs, / And sunset . . ."), the colors of the earth, and the pleasant company of loved ones and friends. Through the senses— the sound of music, the sight of movement, the touch of "flowers and furs and cheeks"—existence is rendered at once tangible and universal as Brooke pulls his images from a common fund of experience.

The octet ends, however, with the senses' death—"All this is ended." Death puts a stop to these pleasurable activities, and the experiences that had constituted the soldiers' identities in life have now lost their significance. The senses are replaced, however, by a new series of symbols from nature. The dead soldiers are compared to the effect of frost that "stays the waves that dance," to "wandering loveliness," and to waters "blown by changing winds to laughter." Death is a transformation into "a white / Unbroken glory, a gathered radiance. . . ." In death, men are no longer defined by their experience of nature but have become part of nature itself.

"The Dead" (II) has met with mixed critical reaction. While some critics admire the poem for its delicate rendering of death as a pristine reincarnation in nature, others have rejected what they see as yet another instance of Brooke sentimentalizing and valorizing death. John Lehmann has expressed his disappointment with the last two lines of the sonnet, noting that "one can only register astonishment that Brooke, who could be so precise when he liked, can crowd so many nouns denoting vaguely emotive general concepts, 'unbroken glory,' 'gathered radiance,' 'shining peace' into two lines." Critic John Johnston has observed with dismay, "The rich images and delicate music of this sonnet constitute something of an achievement in poetic technique, but that achievement is strangely out of contact with the actuality that inspired it." Brooke's heightened idealism, Johnston continues, employs symbols that are too "consciously elegant" and "ingenious" to capture the full implications of death in battle. ❀

Critical Views on
"1914: III. The Dead" and
"1914: IV. The Dead"

CHRISTOPHER HASSALL ON THE YOUNG RUPERT BROOKE

[Christopher Hassall was a distinguished poet, playwright, and biographer. His poetic works include *The Slow Night* and *The Red Leaf*. As a biographer, Hassall is best known for *Edward Marsh: Patron of the Arts* (1959). In this excerpt from his 1964 biography of Rupert Brooke, Hassall examines Brooke's "untidy" posthumous reputation that canonized his war sonnets while ensuring that an aura of "quaintness" forever surrounds his work.]

As the years passed there was much speculation as to what would have happened if Brooke had lived. E. M. Forster was not sure he would have increased his reputation as a poet. He would certainly have become 'a live wire in public affairs and an energetic and enlightened administrator. He had the necessary mixture of toughness and idealism.' Virginia Woolf thought much the same. She knew of people who had returned Brooke's manifest disapproval. 'In fact Bloomsbury was against him and he against them,' she wrote to Gwen Raverat in 1925:

> Meanwhile I had a private version of him which I stuck to when they all cried him down and still preserve somewhere infinitely far away—but how these feelings last, how they come over one, oddly, at unexpected moments—based on my week at Grantchester, when he was all that could be kind and interesting, substantial and good-hearted. (I choose these words without thinking whether they correspond to what he was to you or anybody.) He was, I thought, the ablest of the young men; I didn't think then much of his poetry, which he read aloud on the lawn, but I thought he would be Prime Minister, because he had such a gift with people, and such sanity and force; I remember a weakly pair of lovers meandering in one day, just engaged, very floppy. You know how intense and silly and offhand in a self-conscious way the Cambridge young then were about their loves—Rupert simplified them, and broadened them, humanized them. And then he rode off on a bicycle about a railway strike. My idea was that he was to be a member of Parliament and edit the classics, a very powerful, ambitious man, but not a poet.

She did not share the popular view of the war poems, recalling that they had seemed to her mere 'barrel-organ music,' while the earlier pieces 'were all adjectives and contortions, weren't they?'

What did she mean by contortions? By an odd coincidence, one of those lovers whom Mrs. Woolf describes as meandering into the Old Vicarage when she was staying there, was A. Y. Campbell, who had played the Elder Brother in *Comus,* himself a poet with a turn of wit, and there exists a parody of his on Brooke's early manner which illustrates Mrs. Woolf's point. The parody called *The Voice,* was preserved among Brooke's papers. He evidently enjoyed it. 'With festering hearts that yearn for shadowy night,' it begins, 'We will creep out, a very little way.' It transpires that 'they' hope to reach a wan land far from the cruel day. 'God will be there, of course, and tedious Time, And pale Eternity, that long long thing . . .'

> Occasionally I shall change my tune:
> I'll crack the stars, kick God, and splosh the skies.
> I'll sing of lute-players Rossetti-wise
> Or pull sad faces at the pulpy moon.

Such was the critical view of some contemporaries, and perhaps in 1925, when Mrs. Woolf was writing her letter, she was too close to her own past, too distracted by the major poetical events around her, to look back and observe how far Brooke in his short span developed and purified his style. By this time a new tradition more proper to the age was gaining ground; pre-war verse, written before Armageddon, seemed even more remote than it was, its concerns uninteresting, its manner dated. Brooke, once such a very 'new-fangled young man,' had become un-modern; a movement he was associated with at the start, having lost its first vigour, lay wide open to attack, and the critics who felt in duty bound to discredit it—no very difficult task—succeeded so well that as time passed they went on to accomplish what they never intended. Where the general reader was concerned they confused him and lost him as a poet of any sort whatever. It is easier now to discriminate.

Just as Brooke introduced a new mode of informality among his friends, which gradually spread and became a feature of that general relaxation of manners which the years of war accelerated, so to the poetry of his time he brought a lightness of touch graced by his metaphysical turn of wit. Like the Cavalier poets, he was a man of public affairs with a lyrical gift, and because he was also in some ways what H. W. Garrod has called 'the average nice young man,' he won popularity without aiming or even wishing for it, expressing under a guise of levity the deeper emotions of a reticent class. He risked more sentiment than ever they would have dared, but almost invariably he seemed to wear a smile, said little to which the general heart could not easily respond, and by virtue of his wit, succeeded in making poetry out of that light understatement that Englishmen used to reserve for the things they took most seriously. More than anything else, it is this grace of sociability, so natural to Brooke, which makes him seem old-fashioned. The magnanimous view, an evident zeal to win over, communicate, and share, can hardly be said to be characteristic of a modern poet. Perhaps there is good reason, but perhaps, too, it is a loss to poetry.

Brooke's reputation is an untidy one. He would never have been embarrassed with it had he not been a poet, yet it is not for his poetry itself that he is so widely known. He is a writer apt to be 'known' first and read afterwards, the wrong way round for an author of serious pretensions. While still developing, and preoccupied with what we would be able to call a passing phase, had he not himself passed with it, the lot was his to be made a national figure and have greatness thrust upon him. There he remains, fixed in the public mind, caught in the act of making a superb but not very characteristic gesture. His death at once placed his poetical reputation at the farthest remove from that of, say, Housman, whose secure place in literature has always been as tidy as one of his own stanzas. The works of any one man react upon each other, and his life, if in any way conspicuous, reacts upon them all. So Brooke is remembered as the author of the war sonnets, and it is as if one should characterize Wordsworth by *The Happy Warrior;* and the zeal of his less critical admirers has projected on his public image a sentimental gloss. A kind of patina of 'quaintness' has grown over it; but 'quaintness,' said Brooke himself, 'which swathes dead books as sentimentality swathes dead people, has little hold on the living.'

—Christopher Hassall, *Rupert Brooke* (New York: Harcourt, Brace and World, 1964): pp. 528–31.

ROBERT PEARSALL ON THE PHILOSOPHY OF THE 1914 SONNETS

[Robert Pearsall is professor of English at the College of Notre Dame in California and the author of numerous works, including, *The Californians: Past and Present* (1959), *Robert Browning* (1972), *The Life and Writings of Ernest Hemingway* (1972), and *Rupert Brooke: The Man and Poet* (1974). In this excerpt, Pearsall suggests that despite obvious inconsistencies, the war sonnets are thematically united by their philosophy of death over life.]

The argument of these sonnets as "philosophy" is vaguely harmonious. Taken together, they speak for death over life. Their free-floating main source was to be found in Platonic philosophy, Christian dogmatics, and previous versifications of the patriotic impulse; and specific lines and phrases were drawn from Donne, Browning, Thomas Hardy, and Hilaire Belloc, and from notes made by Brooke himself years earlier, for other uses. Their reasoning simply collapses when referred to any intellectual test, even the test of consistency. Thus the life which is sacrificially abandoned is displayed as beautiful and happy in three poems, "The Dead" going so far as to praise even that old horror of Brooke's, the "unhoped serene / That men call age." By this means the principle of sacrifice is emphasized; the dead have abandoned great treasures. In "The Treasure," however, all the experience of this life is unwrapped again in the next, so that nothing is lost. In "Safety" the paradoxical idea that death protects man from all evils, not excepting "death's endeavor," similarly cancels out sacrifice. In "Peace," the most belligerent of these poems, the world left behind is shown as terrible, and the dead who leave it as lucky to get away—

> as swimmers leaping
> Glad from a world grown old and cold and weary,
> Leave the sick hearts that honour could not move,
> And half-men, and their dirty songs and dreary,
> And all the little emptiness of love.

So in these later three sonnets the death of a soldier becomes an advantage. The concept of sacrifice is therefore muddled even as regards the world supposed to be left behind.

A similar muddledness characterizes the future into which the dead proceed. "The Dead (II)" handles this important matter with beautiful and precise imagery. The dead in that sonnet drop away from color, motion, and warmth, and in a manner turn solid:

> There are waters blown by changing winds to laughter
> And lit by the rich skies, all day. And after,
> > Frost, with a gesture, stays the waves that dance
> And wandering loveliness. He leaves a white
> > Unbroken glory, a gathered radiance,
> A width, a shining peace, under the night.

In "The Treasure" and "The Soldier" death hardly occurs, since the new existence retains the best of the old, or possibly all of it. The speaker in the first of these dies into "some golden space," losing color, light, dancing girls, and birdsong in the old existence, only to find it in the new:

> [There] I'll unpack that scented store
> Of song and flower and sky and face,
> > And count, and touch, and turn them o'er.

In "The Soldier," most famous of all these sonnets, everybody wins. "The corner of a foreign field / That is forever England" is improved because of the "richer dust" buried there. But the original existence, called "heart," is not lost. It still beats, with "all evil shed away," as "pulse in the eternal mind." In "The Dead (I)" the new world of the dead becomes abstractions: Holiness, Honor, Love, Nobleness, and oddly, Pain. In "Safety" it becomes just safety, a term used four times in company with four synonyms meaning the same. Only in "Peace," where the world of the living is so ugly and evil, does the idea of extinction really suffice as the idea of death. "Peace" contains some verbal bargains, especially in the sestet, and its conclusion—"the worst friend and enemy is but death"—holds all that is worst in sentimental mysticism. However, this poem is alone in presenting a harmonious and self-consistent general plan of here and hereafter.

Seeing the poems in proof, Brooke commented "God, they're in the rough, these five camp-children of mine." In his view "The Dead (II)" and "The Soldier" were best, a view probably based on the beautiful sestet of "The Dead (II)" and that celebrated octet of "The Soldier" which has stirred the emotions of people all over the world.

In these sonnets about England he had managed to avoid mentioning cities, railroads, economic affairs, and the dole, filling out the gaps with the landscape data and friendship data of his old resource. His letters as he approached extinction had become filled with wistful references to marriage and children. Passing over the women he loved more and the women he liked more, he asked Katherine Cox to look after one or two business matters he would have to leave unfinished. "I'm telling the Ranee that after she's dead, you're to have my papers. They may want to write a biography! How am I to know if I shan't be eminent?" He had commenced this letter, "I suppose you're about the best I can do in the way of a widow." "The Dead (I)"—"Blow out, you bugles"—has a newer preoccupation in its regret not only for soldiers killed but for "those who would have been / Their sons . . . their immortality."

—Robert Brainard Pearsall, *Rupert Brooke: The Man and Poet* (Amsterdam: Rodopi N.V., 1974): pp. 148–50.

VIRGINIA WOOLF REMEMBERS RUPERT BROOKE

[Virginia Woolf was one of the great Modernist writers, combining a passion for language with a keen sensitivity to the social questions of the day. Among her many books are *To the Lighthouse* (1927), *Orlando* (1928), *Mrs. Dalloway* (1925), and *The Common Reader* (1925). In this excerpt from an unsigned 1918 review of *The Collected Poems of Rupert Brooke,* Woolf recalls the Rupert Brooke she knew—not merely the mythic martyr—as a young man and aspiring poet.]

This memoir of Rupert Brooke has been delayed, in Mrs. Brooke's words, because of "my great desire to obtain the collaboration of some of his contemporaries at Cambridge and during his young manhood, for I strongly believe that they knew the largest part of him." But his contemporaries are for the most part scattered or dead; and though Mr. Marsh has done all that ability or care can do, the memoir which now appears is "of necessity incomplete." It is inevitably incomplete, as Mr. Marsh, we are sure, would be the first to agree, if for no other reason because it is the work of an older man. A single sentence brings this clearly before us. No undergraduate of Rupert Brooke's own age would have seen "his radiant youthful figure in gold and vivid red and blue, like a page in the Riccardi Chapel"; that is the impression of an older man. The contemporary version would have been less pictorial and lacking in the half-humorous tenderness which is so natural an element in the mature vision of beautiful and gifted youth. There would have been less of the vivid red and blue and gold, more that was mixed, particoloured, and matter for serious debate. In addition Mr. Marsh has had to face the enormous difficulties which beset the biographers of those who have died with undeveloped powers, tragically, and in the glory of public gratitude. They leave so little behind them that can serve to recall them with any exactitude. A few letters, written from school and college, a fragment of a diary—that is all. The power of expressing oneself naturally in letters comes to most people late in life. Rupert Brooke wrote freely, but not altogether without self-consciousness, and it is evident that his friends have not cared to publish the more intimate passages in his letters to them. Inevitably, too, they have not been willing to tell the public the informal things by which they remember him best. With these serious and necessary drawbacks Mr. Marsh has done his best to present a general survey of Rupert Brooke's life which those who knew him will be able to fill in here and there more fully, perhaps a little to the detriment of the composition as a whole. But they will be left, we believe, to reflect rather sadly upon the incomplete version which must in future represent Rupert Brooke to those who never knew him.

Nothing, it is true, but his own life prolonged to the usual term, and the work that he would have done, could have expressed all that was latent in the crowded years of his youth—years crowded beyond the measure that is usual even with the young. To have seen a little of him at that time was to have seen enough to be made sceptical of the possibility of any biography of a man dying, as he died, at the age of twenty-eight. The remembrance of a week spent in his company, of a few meetings in London and the country, offers a tantalizing fund of memories at once very definite, very little related to the Rupert Brooke of legend, presenting each one an extremely clear sense of his presence, but depending so much upon that presence and upon other circumstances inextricably involved with it, that one may well despair of rendering a clear account to a third person, let alone to a multiple of many people such as the general public. ⟨. . .⟩

Analyse it as one may, the whole effect of Rupert Brooke in those days was a compound of vigour and of great sensitiveness. Like most sensitive people, he had his methods of self-protection; his pretence now to be this and now to be that. But, however sunburnt and slap-dash he might choose to appear at any particular moment, no one could know him even slightly without seeing that he was not only very sincere, but passionately in earnest about the things he cared for. In particular, he cared for literature and the art of writing as seriously as it is possible to care for them. He had read everything and he had read it from the point of view of a working writer. As Mrs. Cornford says, "I can't imagine him using a word of that emotional jargon in which people usually talk or write of poetry. He made it feel more like carpentering." In discussing the work of living writers he gave you the impression that he had the poem or the story before his eyes in a concrete shape, and his judgments were not only very definite but had a freedom and a reality which mark the criticism of these who are themselves working in the same art. You felt that to him literature was not dead nor of the past, but a thing now in process of construction by people many of whom were his friends; and that knowledge, skill, and, above-all, unceasing hard work were required of those who attempt to make it. To work hard, much harder than most writers think it necessary, was an injunction of his that remains in memory from a chaos of such discussions.

The proofs of his first book of poems were lying about that summer on the grass. There were also the manuscripts of poems that were in the process of composition. It seemed natural to turn his poetry over and say nothing about it, save perhaps to remark upon his habit of leaving spaces for unforthcoming words which gave his manuscript the look of a puzzle with a number of pieces missing. On one occasion he wished to know what was the brightest thing in nature? and then, deciding with a glance round him that the brightest thing was a leaf in the sun, a blank space towards the end of "Town and Country" was filled in immediately.

Cloud-like we lean and stare as bright leaves stare.

But instead of framing any opinion as to the merit of his verses we recall merely the curiosity of watching him finding his adjectives, and a vague conception that he was somehow a mixture of scholar and man of action, and that his poetry was the brilliant by-product of energies not yet turned upon their object. It may seem strange, now that he is famous as a poet, how little it seamed to matter in those days whether he wrote poetry or not. It is proof perhaps of the exciting variety of his gifts and of the immediate impression he made of a being so complete and remarkable in himself that it was sufficient to think of him merely as Rupert Brooke. It was not necessary to imagine him dedicated to any particular pursuit. If one traced a career of him many different paths seemed the proper channels for his store of vitality; but clearly he must find scope for his extraordinary gift of being on good terms with his fellow-creatures. For though it is true to say that "he never 'put himself forward' and seldom took the lead in conversation," his manner shed a friendliness wherever he happened to be that fell upon all kinds of different people, and seemed to foretell that he would find his outlet in leading varieties of men as he had led his own circle of Cambridge friends. His practical ability, which was often a support to his friends, was one of the gifts that seemed to mark him for success in active life. He was keenly aware of the state of public affairs, and if you chanced to meet him when there was talk of a strike or an industrial dispute he was evidently as well versed in the complications of social questions as in the obscurities of the poetry of Donne. There, too, he showed his power of being in sympathy with the present. Nothing of this is in the least destructive of his possession of poetic power. No breadth of sympathy or keenness of susceptibility could come amiss to the writer; but perhaps if one feared for him at all it was lest the pull of all his gifts in their different directions might somehow rend him asunder. He was, as he said of himself, "forty times as sensitive as anybody else," and apt, as he wrote, to begin "poking at his own soul, examining it, cutting the soft and rotten parts away." It needed no special intimacy to guess that beneath "an appearance almost of placidity" he was the most restless, complex, and analytic of human beings. It was impossible to think of him withdrawn, abstracted, or indifferent. Whether or not it was for the good of his poetry he would be in the thick of things, and one fancies that he would in the end have framed a speech that came very close to the modern point of view—a subtle analytic poetry, or prose perhaps, full of intellect, and full of his keen unsentimental curiosity.

No one could have doubted that as soon as war broke out he would go without hesitation to enlist. His death and burial on the Greek island, which "must ever be shining with his glory that we buried there," was in harmony with his physical splendour and with the generous warmth of his spirit. But to imagine him entombed, however nobly and fitly, apart form our interests and passions still seems impossibly incongruous with what we remember of his inquisitive eagerness about life, his response to every side of it, and his complex power, at once so appreciative and so sceptical, of testing and enjoying, of suffering and taking with the utmost sharpness the impression of everything that came his way. One turns from the thought of him not with a sense of completeness and finality, but rather to wonder and to question still: what would he have been, what would he have done?

—Virginia Woolf, Review of *The Collected Poems of Rupert Brooke,* *The Times Literary Supplement* (8 August 1918).

Thematic Analysis of
"1914: V. The Soldier"

"The Soldier" is perhaps Rupert Brooke's best-known and loved work and may be the most famous single poem of the war. The 1914 sonnets, written during November and December of that year and published in a periodical called *New Numbers,* were not widely read at first. But then on Easter Sunday 1915, Dean Inge, preaching in St. Paul's, read "The Soldier" to his congregation and announced that, "the enthusiasm of a pure and elevated patriotism had never found a nobler expression." The poem was reprinted in *The Times,* generating considerable interest. When, about a week later, news came of Brooke's death in the Aegean, the initial words of the poem, "If I should die," gained a prophetic quality. This cluster of events combined to launch Brooke's status as a national hero and martyr.

Of all the war sonnets, "The Soldier" is the only one containing the first person singular. Thus in spite of the self-effacement implied in the first lines—"If I should die, think only this of me: / That there's some corner of a foreign field / That is for ever England"—Brooke here is dramatizing the tragedy of his own possible death. The remaining lines of the octet paint the picture of the England that Brooke had grown up with and loved. Pastoral, unspoiled, and pure, this England represents all that Brooke felt the war was fighting to defend. The tenderness and care with which he traces his memory of all he loves about his country, whose name he repeatedly invokes, also serves to underscore the enormity of the sacrifice he feels he is willing to make. "A dust whom England bore, shaped, made aware, / Gave, once, her flowers to love, her ways to roam, / A body of England's, breathing English air, / Washed by the rivers, blest by suns of home."

Brooke also presented this same theme of sacrifice in an article entitled "An Unusual Young Man," written in early August 1914 and published in *The New Statesman.* Although some of the personal information is changed and the third-person pronoun is used, Brooke himself is the man in question. In the article, he is pictured on a beach in Cornwall when news arrives of the declaration of war. The man's thoughts drift back to his experiences among those people now declared his enemy. Although he remembers with fondness a night of poetic drunkenness with young Germans in Munich, he returns to the word England, which "seemed to flash like a line of foam." He becomes aware of that same duality in his mind he had encountered before: one half dashing erratically from thought to thought, the lower half laboring with some "profound and unknowable change." He continues:

> With a sudden tightening of his heart, he realized that there might be a raid on the English coast. He didn't imagine any possibility of its *succeeding*, but only of enemies and warfare on English soil. The idea sickened him. He was immensely surprised to perceive that the actual earth of England held for him a quality which he found in A— [his lover], and in a friend's honour, and scarcely anywhere else, a quality which, if he'd ever been sentimental enough to use the word, he'd have called "holiness." His astonishment grew as the full flood of "England" swept him on from thought to thought. He felt the triumphant helplessness of a lover.

What makes this man unusual is his admission that in this moment of general disaster, "At the same time he was extraordinarily happy." He does not shy away from the horrors of war, easily imagining how he might have to kill those he formerly considered friends. But his discovery of something higher and bigger than himself, a cause, as Christopher Hassall notes, "that could never let him down, even if it ended in defeat," overwhelmed whatever sense of trepidation or doubt he might have.

In the sestet of "The Soldier," we learn why this sacrifice can be so willingly given. In spite of death, the original existence, the "heart," of the soldier is not lost. It has merely been purified, "all evil shed away," and now beats as "pulse in the eternal mind." In this death, the soldier has found a way of bequeathing his possessions—his memories of his beloved England—to future generations to enjoy. These are "Her sights and sounds; dreams happy as her day; / And laughter, learnt of friends; and gentleness, / In hearts at peace."

Preserving this pure and unsullied vision of England, then, has become the soldier's sacred duty and solemn token of thanks. By identifying his own body and the soil of England in an almost mystical fashion, Brooke ensures that both he and England will transcend death and national boundaries by achieving immortality in the hearts and minds of English people everywhere.

"The Soldier" completes the *1914* sonnets, ending the series on a note of patriotic self-sacrifice and determined steadfastness. More recent critics have complained that "The Soldier" is "riddled with sentimentality and narcissistic fantasy," but there is no denying that this poem has struck a chord with readers ever since its publication. ✸

Critical Views on
"1914: V. The Soldier"

WINSTON CHURCHILL ON ONE OF ENGLAND'S
"NOBLEST SONS"

[Winston Churchill (1874–1965) was one of the great soldiers, statesmen, and historians of his day. In addition to serving as prime minister of Great Britain (1940–45), he was also the winner of a coveted Nobel Prize for Literature in 1953. His works include *The World Crisis* (1923–31), *Marlborough: His Life and Times* (1933–38), *The Second World War* (1948–54), and *The History of English-Speaking Peoples* (1956–61). In this valediction for Brooke published in *The Times* on April 26, 1915, as first reports from the Gallipoli landing were being expected, Churchill laid the foundation for the national myth of Rupert Brooke. Churchill glorified the sacrifice of a life so full of promise, extolling him for being "all that one would wish England's noblest sons to be in days when no sacrifice but the most precious is acceptable."]

"W. S. C." writes:—"Rupert Brooke is dead. A telegram from the Admiral at Lemnos tell us that this life has closed at the moment when it seemed to have reached its springtime. A voice had become audible, a note had been struck, more true, more thrilling, more able to do justice to the nobility of our youth in arms engaged in this present war, than any other—more able to express their thoughts of self-surrender, and with a power to carry comfort to those who watch them so intently from afar. The voice has been swiftly stilled. Only the echoes and the memory remain; but they will linger.

"During the last few months of his life, months of preparation in gallant comradeship and open air, the poet-soldier told with all the simple force of genius the sorrow of youth about to die, and the sure triumphant consolations of a sincere and valiant spirit. He expected to die; he was willing to die for the dear England whose beauty and majesty he knew; and he advanced towards the brink in perfect serenity, with absolute conviction of the rightness of his country's cause and a heart devoid of hate for fellow-men.

"The thoughts to which he gave expression in the very few incomparable war sonnets which he has left behind will be shared by many thousands of young men moving resolutely and blithely forward into this, the hardest, the cruellest, and the least-rewarded of all the wars that men have fought. They are a whole history and revelation of Rupert Brooke himself. Joyous, fearless, versatile, deeply instructed, with classic symmetry of mind and body, ruled by high undoubting purpose, he was all that one would wish England's noblest sons to be in days when no sacrifice but the most precious is acceptable, and the most precious is that which is most freely proffered."

—Winston Churchill, "Death of Mr. Rupert Brooke," *The Times* (26 April 1915): p. 5.

ARTHUR STRINGER ON MOURNING RUPERT BROOKE

[Arthur Stringer was a prolific and popular Canadian poet, novelist, critic, and biographer, author of works such as *The Silver Poppy* (1903), *The Prairie Wife* (1915), *The Prairie Mother* (1920), *The Prairie Child* (1922), *A Lady Quite Lost* (1929), *A Woman at Dusk, and Other Poems* (1928), *The Old Woman Remembers, and Other Irish Poems* (1938), and *The King Who Loved Old Clothes and Other Irish Poems* (1941). This excerpt from Stringer's sentimental 1948 biography of the poet, *Red Wine of Youth: A Life of Rupert Brooke*, gives a sense of the melodramatic longing and loss that accompanied Brooke's death and subsequent canonization.]

Closer to home the expressions of sorrow were even more prompt and poignant. In that year which hung so dark over England and in those days of bitter conflict when life was so cheap Rupert's preoccupied countrymen paused to mourn for their lost singer. Not since the death of Byron at Missolonghi had the passing of a soldier-poet so moved the hearts of a nation.

At Rugby, where Rupert was remembered as a golden-haired youth and revered as a golden-voiced lyrist, a memorial service took place in the school chapel where he had so often sung at vespers. There Sir Ian Hamilton unveiled a marble portrait medallion on which was inscribed "Rupert Brooke, 1887-1915" and under that name and date the well-know lines of "The Soldier" sonnet:

> If I should die, think only this of me:
> That there's some corner of a foreign field
> That is for ever England. There shall be
> In that rich earth a richer dust concealed;
> A dust whom England bore, shaped, made aware,
> Gave, once, her flowers to love, her ways to roam,
> A body of England's, breathing English air,
> Washed by the rivers, blest by suns of home. . . .

In a moving address the war-scarred general, after being received by a guard of honor made up of youthful members of the School O.T.C. (in which Rupert had once proudly marched) paid fitting tribute to a younger man who was, like himself, both a soldier and a poet. A part of his address as reported in the Rugby *Observer* is as follows:

"We have come together to this School where Rupert Brooke lived and was best known, to tender our homage to his memory. Is it because he was a hero? There were others. But Rupert Brooke held all three gifts of the gods in his hand. He held them in his hand only to fling them eagerly down, as if they were three common little dice. He cast the dice, but Death had loaded them. . . . I went into his tent, where he was lying stretched out on the desert sand, looking extraordinarily handsome, a very knightly presence. Whilst speaking to him my previous fears crystalised into a sudden strong premonition that he was one of those whom the envious gods loved too well. So I made my futile effort and begged him to come to my personal staff, where I would see to it he would get serious work to do. I knew the temper of his spirit and I promised him a fair share of danger.

"He replied just as Sir Philip Sydney would have replied. He would have loved to come, he said, but he loved better the thought of going through with the first landing and the first and worst fighting, shoulder to shoulder with his comrades.

"He was right. There was nothing more to be said. And so on the afternoon of the 23rd of April when the black ships lay thick on the wonderful blue of the Bay and the troops in their transports steamed slowly out, cheering, wild with enthusiasm and joy, Rupert Brooke lay dying. . . ."

After that address the prayer of dedication was offered by the headmaster of Rugby, followed by a reading of the third chapter of Ephesians, from the same pulpit where Dr. Thomas Arnold had once delivered his historic sermons. Then, led by the organ the dead Denis Browne had loved to play of a winter afternoon, the gathering united in singing the National Anthem.

In that gathering was the poet's mother and his trusted and often-tried friend Edward Marsh. With them was Walter de la Mare and Lascelles Abercombie and Geoffrey Keynes and the black-clad sister of Cleg Kelly, who before his own death had been moved to compose a proudly mournful "Elegy for Strings" for the comrade he had helped bury in far-off Skyros.

Sitting in one of the chapel pews in the mellowed light from the stained-glass windows was a fellow poet, silent and stoic as ever. There Wilfrid Gibson must have lost himself in memories of earlier days when he and his dead friend had roamed the fields of England and found song in their shared love of life. He knew that a comrade voice had been silenced, that a warm and ardent spirit had slipped away into the Unknown. But that passing, he remembered, was not without its gleam of splendor, for of it he was able to write:

> He's gone.
> I do not understand.
> I only know
> That, as he turned to go
> And waved his hand,
> In his young eyes a sudden glory shone,
> And I was dazzled by a sunset glow—
> And he was gone.

> —Arthur Stringer, *Red Wine of Youth: A Life of Rupert Brooke* (New York: Bobbs-Merrill, 1948): pp. 269–71.

JON SILKIN ON BROOKE IN THE PUBLIC SERVICE

[In this selection from *Out of Battle* (1972), Silkin suggests that part of the reason Brooke's legacy has been so contested lies not in his poetry but in the way his words would be later enlisted for the "needs of the nation."]

Brooke's sonnets are 'war poems'—'The Soldier,' especially—in the sense that they are vehicles for imperialist attitudes. But to see how little they are to do with war in the overt sense one might compare 'If I should die, think only this of me,' not with any of Sassoon's or Owen's war poems, which is too easy a comparison, but with Kipling's 'The Islanders.' It is fair to say that this is, as Brooke's sonnets purport to be, a defense of war's necessity, or at least a plea for the waging of efficient war, given its necessity. The contrast is significant. Brooke's poems begin with the context of war, but move into a peaceful idealization of the sacrifice pending its immortality. Death in a aura of public sympathy, but underlying approval, provides the ennobling quality that was privately satisfying. Any conscience or pain he may be caused by having ceased to be a poet is equalized by his ennobling example and by his preparedness for death. When Brooke learned he was being sent with the Royal Naval Division to Gallipoli, he wrote to Violet Asquith: 'I've never been quite so happy in my life, I think. Not quite so *pervasively* happy; like a stream flowing entirely to one end.' The tragic meaning possible here is of an unconscious adherence to public service and death, used to dissolve those personal problems with which he had been racked. This may be read as selflessness, but it is an abnegation in which personal responsibility has been dissolved. And perhaps this is what the argument over Brooke is about. In a sense it was not his fault, since however much one detests the chauvinistic angelicizing of the soldier killed in battle, it was never his intention to send millions to their death. His mission may have been to make such a death seem more noble, but not to bring about wholesale slaughter; Brooke was far too kind a man for that. He was perhaps not intelligent enough to have grasped the possible dimensions of the struggle, and probably too enfolded in his own sensations to learn from the experience, even when immersed in it. In the middle of the chaos of the Belgian retreat he is able to speak of it as 'an extraordinary and thrilling confusion.' This was not war-mongering, but, unfortunately for him and for other victims of the war, cleverer and more adroit persons capitalized both on his published sentiments (which in any case expressed the feelings of a good many people) and then his example; and used them as instruments for 'speeding glum heroes up the line to death.' One might consider the sequence of events. Brooke saw little action; with a now easily perceived irony he died, on 23 April 1915, from a mosquito bite that developed into septicaemia. The sonnets had been published in the December 1914 issue of *New Numbers*. On 5 April 1915, Easter Sunday, the Dean of St. Paul's preached to a

> congregation [consisting] of widows, parents, and orphans in their hundreds. As the Dean reached the pulpit, a man jumped to his feet and began a loud harangue against the war. When he was removed, Dean Inge gave as his text, Isaiah XXVI, 19. *The dead shall live, my dead bodies shall arise. Awake and sing, ye that dwell in the dust.* He had just read ['The Soldier'] . . . and remarked that 'the enthusiasm of a pure and elevated patriotism had never found a nobler expression.'

At once, with the help of the war, Dean Inge, and even the man who had made his protest, Brooke became famous; and in a way that not all the combined publicity of Marsh and the Georgian anthologies had managed. There are several ironies here, but the principal one is that despite his flair for publicity, nothing of this, except the writing of the poems, was Brooke's doing. With the Church's erastian complicity he was canonized for the 'needs of the nation,' and used as an instrument to promote further slaughter.

—Jon Silkin, *Out of Battle: The Poetry of the Great War,* 2nd ed. (London: Macmillan, 1998): pp. 67–69.

Biography of
Siegfried Sassoon

Siegfried Sassoon (1886–1967) is best remembered for his angry and satirical poems of the First World War. Evoking the soul-wrenching terror and brutality of trench warfare, Sassoon vigorously denounced generals, politicians, and churchmen for their incompetence and blind support of the war. Although Sassoon continued to write after the war, his later poems, which were often concerned with religious themes, received less critical acclaim than his war poems.

Sassoon was born into a wealthy Jewish family in Kent. He lived the easy life of a cultivated country gentleman before the First World War, pursuing his two major interests, poetry and fox hunting. His early work, which was privately printed in several slim volumes between 1906 and 1916, is considered minor and imitative, heavily influenced by the poet John Masefield. His 1913 *The Daffodil Murderer,* a clever parody of Masefield's realistic narratives, was his first success, albeit a minor one. Sasooon received encouragement from Edmund Gosse, a family friend, and Edward Marsh. These two influential literary pundits initiated Sassoon into the Georgian literary and artistic world.

Sassoon first saw action in late 1915, serving with the Royal Welsh Fusiliers; the same year, he received a Military Cross for bringing back a wounded soldier during heavy fire. After being wounded in action, he had the opportunity to meet with other pacifists, including Bertrand Russell and H. G. Wells; as a result, Sassoon wrote an open letter of protest to the war department, refusing to fight any more. "I believe that this War is being deliberately prolonged by those who have the power to end it," he wrote in the letter.

In his memoir of those years, *Siegfried's Journey 1916–1920,* Sassoon recalls an evening when he reflected on what he was about to do.

> I sat alone in the club library with a fair copy of the "statement" before me on the writing-table. The words were now solidified and unalterable. My brain was unable to scrutinize their meaning any more. They had become merely a sequence of declamatory sentences,

designed to let me in for what appeared to be a moral equivalent of "going over the top"; and, at the moment, the Hindenburg Line felt preferable in retrospect. For the first time, I allowed myself to reflect upon the consequences of my action and to question my strength to endure them. Possibly what I disliked most was the prospect of being misunderstood and disapproved of by my fellow officers. Some of them would regard my behaviour as a disgrace to the regiment. Others would assume that I had gone a bit crazy. How many of them, I wondered, would give me credit for having done it for the sake of the troops who were at the Front?

At the urging of Russell, the letter was read in the House of Commons; it was also printed in the London *Times*. Sassoon expected to be court-martialed for his protest, but poet Robert Graves intervened on his behalf, arguing that Sassoon was suffering from shellshock and needed medical treatment. In 1917, Sassoon was hospitalized at Craiglockhart near Edinburgh.

At Craiglockhart Sassoon wrote the poems that would be published in *Counter-Attack* in 1918. He also befriended a young officer patient who wrote poetry—Wilfred Owen. But Sassoon refused to stay at Craiglockhart for long. As he was not really suffering from shellshock, he felt he was betraying his fellow soldiers. By early January 1918, Sassoon was back in active duty.

In May he and his battalion were rushed to France. On July 13, Sassoon, returning from a patrol through no-man's land, was shot in the head—one of his own sergeants had mistaken him for a German. The war ended before Sassoon saw any more fighting.

Public reaction to Sassoon's poetry was fierce. Some readers complained that the poet displayed little patriotism, while others found his shockingly realistic depiction of war to be too extreme. Even pacifist friends complained about the violence and graphic detail in his work. But the British public bought the books because, in his best poems, Sassoon captured the feeling of trench warfare and the weariness of British soldiers. By the time *Counter-Attack* appeared, the public mood was ready for what he had to say.

Even Winston Churchill, then Minister of Munitions, admired these poems and even learned some of them by heart. Rather than viewing them as anti-war propaganda, however, Churchill felt the poems would bring home to the civilian population what the troops at the Front had to endure. "The dynamic quality of his war poems," according to a critic for the *Times Literary Supplement,* "was due to the intensity of feeling which underlay their cynicism." When compared to his friend, Wilfred Owen, however, Sassoon was often found wanting, a conclusion best summed up by Bernard Bergonzi who declared, "He [Sassoon] is usually regarded as a smaller, because less compassionate and universal, poet than Owen."

After the war, Sassoon became involved in Labour Party politics, lectured on pacifism, and continued to write. His most successful works of this period were his trilogy of autobiographical novels, *The Memoirs of George Sherston,* which appeared from 1928–1936. In these, he gave a thinly fictionalized account of his wartime experiences, with little changed except the names, contrasting these experiences with his nostalgic memories of country life before the war and recounting the growth of his pacifist feelings. Sassoon's critical biography of Victorian novelist and poet George Meredith was also well received.

Sassoon married Hester Gatty on December 18, 1933. The marriage was unsuccessful, and the couple separated after 10 years.

In 1957 Sassoon became a convert to Catholicism; for some time before his conversion, religious themes had been the predominant subject of his writing. These later religious poems never achieved the same enthusiastic critical or popular reaction as those written between 1917 and 1920.

Sassoon died in his sleep on September 1, 1967. ✸

Thematic Analysis of
"Enemies"

"Enemies" is one of Siegfried Sassoon's earlier poems, dated January 6, 1917. He wrote it after a day's hunting while he was on leave. Like Owen's "Strange Meeting," "Enemies" confronts the question of the responsibility of killing in war. In the poem, a dead soldier finds himself in Armageddon, the afterworld, where he is confronted by his recently slain enemies. In "Strange Meeting" the narrator faces an enemy whom he himself has killed, but in "Enemies" the "hulking Germans" are killed by another man, as revenge for the death of the soldier. Some critics have seen the poem as a visionary homage to Sassoon's remembered love for David Thomas, who was killed by a stray bullet on March 18, 1916, or for his brother Hamo, who was killed at Gallipoli on November 1, 1915. (According to Robert Graves, Sassoon vowed revenge for Thomas's death and went out every night on voluntary bloodthirsty patrols looking for Germans.)

Throughout Sassoon's writing, one gets a sense of his own growing sense of guilt at the killing he himself had committed. And yet at other times in Sassoon's autobiographical writing, war emerges as the stuff of which poetry is made:

> I used to say I couldn't kill anybody in this war; but since they shot Tommy [Ltn. Thomas] I would gladly stick a bayonet into a German by daylight. Someone told me a year ago that love, sorrow, and hate were things I had never known (things which every poet *should* know!). Now I have known love for Bobbie (Hanmer) and Tommy, and grief for Hamo and Tommy, and hate has come also, and the lust to kill.

The first lines of "Enemies" establish the isolation of the soldier "alone in some queer sunless place." Having already made the passage to the afterlife, the narrator cannot ask him what he thinks about his own death and the carnage around him, but we are encouraged to assume that he feels regret at his life being cut short. Again like "Strange Meeting," "Enemies" is not concerned with the battle itself but with that moment beyond the heat and frenzy of fighting that allows for reflection and revelation. Away from the battle, even the throng of Germans who join him in the afterworld are no longer threatening—they have been rendered "patient, stupid, sullen ghosts of men" by the "brooding rage" of the vengeful narrator. The unperturbed dead soldier and the passive ghosts of his enemies are placed in stark contrast to the enraged narrator.

But while the distant sight of battle seems not to disturb the dead soldier, when confronted with the sight of the Germans killed on his behalf, the implications of the fighting come home to him. A sense of dissonance and incomprehension emerges; he is at once the enemy of these men and yet he shares more in common with them now that he is dead than he does with those still fighting on his behalf. At first, the soldier is at a loss to respond; words themselves are insufficient in the face of death. The customary battle-lines of war that keep enemies apart have been obscured in death, where they are now united as victims. Finally, a smile achieves what words could not, suggesting that a meeting beyond the slaughter and enmity can occur, a meeting not as enemies but as human beings.

Throughout Sassoon's poetry one can find evidence of his near obsessive compassion for his fellow soldiers. This compassion lead him first to his public opposition to the war, and later it brought him to the guilty conviction that only by returning to action and sharing his fellow soldiers' suffering could his dual role as officer and artist be vindicated. In his 1917 anti-war protest, one can see how Sassoon identifies with his men:

> I am making this statement as an act of willful defiance of military authority, because I believe that the War is being deliberately prolonged by those who have the power to end it. I am a soldier, convinced that I am acting on behalf of soldiers. I believe that this War, upon which I entered as a war of defense and liberation, has now become a war of aggression and conquest. I believe that the purposes for which I and my fellow soldiers entered upon this War should have been clearly stated as to have made it impossible for them to be changed without our knowledge, and that, had this been done, the objects which actuated us would now be attainable by negotiation.
>
> I have seen and endured the sufferings of the troops, and I can no longer be a party to prolonging those sufferings for ends which I believe to be evil and unjust.
>
> I am not protesting against the military conduct of the War, but against the political errors and insincerities for which the fighting men are being sacrificed.
>
> On behalf of those who are suffering now, I make this protest against the deception which is being practiced on them. Also I believe that it may help to destroy the callous complacence with which the majority of those at home regard the continuance of

agonies which they do not share, and which they have not sufficient imagination to realise.

Out of concern and compassion for his men, Sassoon took his opposition to the war into the public arena. In the future, he would return to fight in the war not out of some romantic belief in the nobility of sacrifice for one's country but out of a sense of solidarity with his men. Faced with the enormity of death and suffering generated by the war, Sassoon, like the characters in "Enemies," came to understand that the conventional premises of the war, founded in the opposition of "us" versus "them," were arbitrary and ultimately meaningless. The difference between living and dead was the only one that mattered. ❀

Critical Views on
"Enemies"

MICHAEL THORPE ON HUMAN SYMPATHY IN SASSOON'S
WAR POEMS

[Michael Thorpe is the author of numerous books of poetry
as well as several nonfiction works, including *Siegfried
Sassoon: A Critical Study* (1966), *The Poetry of Edmund
Blunden* (1971), and *Doris Lessing's Africa* (1979). He has
also contributed poems, articles, and reviews to such
publications as the London *Times, World Literature Today,
English Studies,* and *Transition.* In this selection from his
critical study of Siegfried Sassoon, Thorpe examines how
Sassoon has been negatively compared to Owen because of
Sassoon's allegedly unrestrained emotionalism.]

The weaknesses of the subjective poems—the rawness of the
emotion and the undisciplined expression of it—mar also most of
the poems of private grief or of compassion for fellow-soldiers,
individually or *en masse.* Seldom is the feeling allowed to work
through, or emerge from, the poem itself. More often, feeling
outruns expression. The hated phenomena of war—the "cursed
wood" that must be stormed, to face death "like a prowling beast"—
too readily become stereotypes that evoke no sharp response. The
men themselves—"the kind, common ones . . . / What stubborn-
hearted virtues they disguised!" ('Conscripts'), "Young Fusiliers,
strong-legged and bold" ('In Barracks')—are sentimentalised. There
is a dangerously high proportion of cliché in the poems of strong
feeling, as if he had not the urge for precision or the artistic
conscience to vary his expression. While in the poems of protest this
roughness serves him well as part of the angry voice almost
inarticulate with the urgency of a message whose audience is
assured, in a poem intended to evoke a deeper response the deadness
of the language dulls the effect. Phrases like "the wild beast of battle"
('Prelude: the Troops'), "dreams that drip with murder"
('Survivors'), and the almost perfunctory metaphorical use of "hell,"
blur the impact of poems in which everything depends on the
intensity of description. 'Prelude' and 'Survivors' have similar
themes, but little of the force of Owen's 'Exposure' and 'Mental

Cases.' Sassoon's pen is too liable to slip over the concrete reality which it is his first duty to communicate and which Owen evokes by both word and rhythm: he rushes instead to press upon the reader his own feelings and his view of what the reader's should be. The "seemingly casual, cliché style" that Blunden justly admires is a two-edged weapon. The clichés that in the satire work by contrast with the overwhelming reality have an artistic justification which their counterparts in the poems of compassion, in vainly seeking to match the reality, cannot share. ⟨. . .⟩

⟨. . .⟩ It has become a critical commonplace to set Sassoon down, as B. Ifor Evans does, as "outstandingly the most effective" writer of the 'realist stage' of War poetry, reserving for Owen the prime place of honour as the poet capable of going deeper than emotional and biassed outbursts (as "Blighters" and 'The Fathers' are biassed) to a quality of pity that is 'not strain'd.' Pinto describes Sassoon's war poetry as "purely destructive," in that it creates nothing with which to rebuild; Johnston, in *English Poetry of the First World War,* shares this view. While one would not quarrel with the essential justice of these judgments (though Pinto's has an exaggerated negative emphasis), any more than Sassoon does in his generous comments on Owen, it can be shown that his response to the War is not confined to angry satire, sentimentality or a morbid preoccupation with his own predicament. A handful (admittedly) of his poems have a moving directness and simplicity which eschews sentimentality or morbidity; on a humbler scale than Owen's they plead human sympathy and understanding.

As with the satirical epigrams, this is best expressed within a brief compass, when he is not consciously striving for the large statement: the praiseworthy poems are 'Two Hundred Years After,' 'The Hawthorn Tree,' 'The Dug-Out,' and, though it is not a perfect whole, 'Enemies'; with some reservations, the longer descriptive pieces, 'Concert Party' and 'Night on the Convoy,' may be added to these. The range of feeling in these poems is wider than that customarily associated with Sassoon.

In the early sonnet 'Two Hundred Years After,' he achieves the physical immediacy and simple expression of feeling that are so often absent from the more sensational Front Line poems. It is cleanly and economically constructed. We are first given a vivid picture of one of the most familiar—and least spectacular—sights of the War, a column drawing the rations up to the Line under cover of darkness. There is no intrusive comment; the picture is allowed to do its own work, to serve as a symbol of the futility of the struggle. This done, it is obliterated from the watcher's gaze by "a rainy scud" and the lights of the village—of normality, of peace-time continuity—appear. The few, compassionate words of the old man who has seen this ghostly scene often have a Hardyan simplicity: "Poor silent things, they were the English dead / Who came to fight in France and got their fill." This is indeed all that is likely to be said: it needed distinctive insight to grasp the enduring meaning of the common scene and poetic tact to point its significance without mawkishness.

Another (surprisingly) early poem, 'Enemies,' is less finished. It begins poorly with the vague "queer sunless place" and the accustomed reference to "Armageddon," but in the crucial part Sassoon avoids the romantic elaboration of 'The Last Meeting' and allows the one he grieves for to be only suggested. The flat simplicity of statement convinces: "One took his hand / Because his face could make them understand"—wisely, there is no attempt to show why this is so. But what matters most is the idea—the meeting of human beings beyond the hatred and the slaughter—a mere sketch, admittedly, for 'Strange Meeting' or even Sorley's sonnet 'To Germany': the link between enemies is far from being forged. One is inclined to wish Sassoon had attempted something more ample on this theme: though it is implicit in his war poetry as a whole that he has no strong anti-German feelings, his failure to crystallise this into a positive attitude exemplifies his limitations.

—Michael Thorpe, *Siegfried Sassoon: A Critical Study* (London: Oxford University Press, 1967): pp. 30–31, 32–33.

JOSEPH COHEN AND THE THREE ROLES OF SASSOON

[Joseph Cohen is a writer and literary columnist who has written for various literary publications in the United States and Canada. He also served as a contributing editor for the *Journal of Higher Education* and as a member of the

Sassoon's enthusiasm for his role of angry prophet is amply recorded in his prose accounts of his war experiences, *The Memoirs of George Sherston* and *Siegfried's Journey 1916–1920;* but the intensity with which he responded to the role and developed it during the war years and afterward is revealed only in his poems. The prose accounts are of emotions recollected in tranquillity; the war poems are the raw unchecked emotions themselves. In the two dozen or so war poems first collected into *The Old Huntsman and Other Poems* published in 1917, Sassoon unleashed the exasperation, the horror, the fear, the disillusionment, and the bitter cynicism that came to characterize the poetry of the trenches in the war's last two years. From the brown rats, sucking clay, droning shells, gray weather, rotten boots, sagging wires, cracking rifles, thundering cannon, and riddled corpses, Sassoon abstracted the futility, despair, loneliness and mockery of the war, and with fury thrust it into the faces of his unsuspecting countrymen, safe and snug in England.

His approach was direct and his technique simple: he emphasized and re-emphasized the contrast between the relative comfort and safety of the homefront and the misery and insecurity of the trenches. While the poetic worth of his formula was questionable, its communicative potential was unlimited. Sassoon exploited, without hesitation, the shock value obtained from exposing the superficial optimism of those whom the people set in authority. The bishop in "They" is a typical target:

> The Bishop tells us: 'When the boys come back
> 'They will not be the same; for they have fought
> 'In a just cause: they lead the last attack
> 'On Anti-Christ; their comrade's blood has bought
> 'New right to breed an honourable race,
> 'They have challenged Death and dared him face to face.'
>
> 'We're none of us the same!' the boys reply.
> 'For George lost both his legs; and Bill's stone blind;
> 'Poor Jim's shot through the lungs and like to die;

'And Bert's gone syphilitic: you'll not find
'A chap who's served that hasn't found *some* change.'
And the Bishop said: "The ways of God are strange!"

In this poem and its companion pieces one finds the requisites of the prophet. Sassoon appears as the enemy of ignorance, complacency, hypocrisy, and sin, the advocate of the poor and oppressed, the leader in social reform. His utterances are enthusiastic and seemingly inspired; his is the voice calling the people away from their wickedness into the paths of truth and righteousness. He possesses something of the mystic whose visions go beyond this world. ⟨. . .⟩

It must be recognized, in retrospect, that Sassoon's war poetry suffered from his indulging too much in the role of prophet, for once he decided that it was proper for him, he entered upon the role with so much exuberance that he permanently hurt his reputation as a poet. True, he pleaded effectively for the combatants and just as effectively castigated those whom he held responsible for the suffering of the soldiers. But his verse pleadings and remonstrances reduced his efforts to political propaganda. Though he foresaw and foretold the misery involved in the prolongation of the war, his rash attacks alienated many whom he might otherwise have induced to accept his point of view. Most of all, he lacked the compassion which gave needed balance and restraint to the works of two other poets of the war, then unknown, Wilfred Owen (whom Sassoon discovered while in hospital), and Osbert Sitwell.

—Joseph Cohen, "The Three Roles of Siegfried Sassoon," *Tulane Studies in English*, vol. 7 (New Orleans: Tulane University, 1957): pp. 170–71, 175.

JOHN MIDDLETON MURRY ON READING SIEGFRIED SASSOON

[British journalist and author John Middleton Murry is best known for his erudite and controversial criticism. He began his career as founder of the avant-garde magazine *Rhythm* in the late 1900s. In 1913 he married writer Katherine Mansfield. With the encouragement of novelist D. H. Lawrence, Murry also published much criticism, including the studies *Fyodor Dostoevsky* (1916) and *The Problem of Style* (1922), which were well received for Murry's original insights. Following Mansfied's death in 1923, Murry wrote *Keats and Shakespeare* (1925), an analysis of Keats that confirmed Murry's reputation as a provocative, emotionally charged critic. From 1923 to 1948 Murry also edited the magazine *Adelphi,* in which he provided a pacifist perspective on global issues. In this selection Murry questions how effective Sassoon was in expressing the full range of human emotion.]

It is the fact, not the poetry, of Mr. Sassoon that is important. When a man is in torment and cries aloud, his cry is incoherent. It has neither weight nor meaning of its own. It is inhuman, and its very inhumanity strikes to the nerve of our hearts. We long to silence the cry, whether by succour and sympathy, or by hiding ourselves from it. That it should somehow stop or be stopped, and by ceasing trouble our hearts no more, is our chief desire; for it is ugly and painful, and it rasps at the cords of nature.

Mr. Sassoon's verses—they are not poetry—are such a cry. They touch not our imagination, but our sense. Reading them, we feel, not as we do with true art, which is the evidence of a man's triumph over his experience, that something has after all been saved from disaster, but that everything is irremediably and intolerably wrong. And, God knows, something is wrong—wrong with Mr. Sassoon, wrong with the world which has made him the instrument of a discord so jangling. Why should one of the finest creatures of the earth be made to suffer a pain so brutal that he can give it no expression, that even this most human and mighty relief is denied him?

For these verses express nothing, save in so far as a cry expresses pain. Their effect is exhausted when the immediate impression dies away. Some of them are, by intention, realistic pictures of battle experience, and indeed one does not doubt their truth. The language is over-wrought, dense and turgid, as a man's mind must be under the stress and obsession of a chaos beyond all comprehension. ⟨. . .⟩

There is a value in the direct transcription of plain, unvarnished fact; but there is another truth more valuable still. One may convey the chaos of immediate sensation by a chaotic expression, as does Mr. Sassoon. But the unforgettable horror of an inhuman experience can only be rightly rendered by rendering also its relation to the harmony and calm of the soul which it shatters. In this context alone can it appear with that sudden shock to the imagination which is overwhelming. The faintest discord in a harmony has within it an infinity of disaster, which no confusion of notes, however wild and various and loud, can possibly suggest. It is on this that the wise saying that poetry is emotion recollected in tranquillity is so firmly based, for the quality of an experience can only be given by reference to the ideal condition of the human consciousness which it disturbs with pleasure or with pain. But in Mr. Sassoon's verses it is we who are left to create for ourselves the harmony of which he gives us only the moment of its annihilation. It is we who must be the poets and the artists if anything enduring is to be made of his work. He gives us only the data. There is, indeed, little enough harm in this; it is good that we should have the data; it is good that Mr. Sassoon should have written his book, and that the world should read it. But our concern here is with Mr. Sassoon the potential poet.

There is a danger that work such as his may pass current as poetry. It has the element of poetical popularity, for it produces an immediate impression. And since Mr. Sassoon is a young man, he may be hypnotised by popularity into believing that his work is done, and may end by wrecking the real poetic gift which at rare intervals peeps out in a line.

> The land where all
> Is ruin and nothing blossoms but the sky.

The last five words are beautiful because they do convey horror to the imagination, and do not bludgeon the senses. They convey horror to the imagination precisely because they contain, as it were, a full octave of emotional experience, and the compass ranges from serenity to desolation, not merely of the earth, but of the mind. The horror is in relation; it is placed, and therefore created. ⟨...⟩

—John Middleton Murry, *The Evolution of an Intellectual* (London: Richard Cobden-Sanderson, 1920): pp. 70–71, 73–75.

Thematic Analysis of
"Conscripts"

"Conscripts" was first published in the *Spectator* on February 17, 1917. It marks a departure from the short, epigrammatic poem that had become Sassoon's preferred form. Instead, "Conscripts" contains five stanzas that describe the drilling of young men at Litherland.

In his diary of December 27, 1916, Sassoon had recorded just such an activity, writing: "Clumsy recruits . . . *On* garrrd! Long-point at the stomach etc. Red-and-black-striped-jersey instructors with well-poised bodies and wasp-waists, moving easily among the bunchy, awkward privates—pathetic crowd of willy-nilly patriots and (?) heroes!"

In the first three stanzas of "Conscripts," a drill-sergeant persona tries to drive out the individuality and frivolousness of his new soldiers. This narrator mocks the ideals and "attractive attitudes" of the soldiers, as he repeatedly scorns their romantic notions. The transition they must make from the idyllic comfort of life before the war and the harsher reality of wartime existence is exemplified by the replacement of their clothes' "luminous rich colours" with uniform khaki. There is nothing romantic about this change. "What's magic got to do with you?" the narrator retorts, "There's no such thing! Blood's red, and skies are blue."

In the second and third stanzas, Sassoon presents the conscripts as personifications of various values cherished before the war—"Love," "Rhyme," "Joy," "Wisdom," "Fancy," "Rapture," "Enchantment," "Romance." This personification serves simultaneously as a reminder of the fragility of these ideals, contained within the hearts and minds of impressionable and very mortal young men, and as a parody of the use of such clichéd tropes in much poetry. These abstract ideals are now linked to the most banal physical situations: "Rhyme got sore heels and wanted to fall out. . ."; "Love chucked his lute away. . ."; "Wisdom gnawed his fingers. . . ." The narrator is an unwilling taskmaster before this group of innocent, unruly children—"how I longed to set them free!"—and his lessons on tactical matters—"Defence, Attack"—seem to leave little mark on his uninterested pupils.

Sassoon himself was reluctant to take on the responsibility of training soldiers. During his convalescence in February 1917, after being wounded in the shoulder while leading his company in an attack on the Somme front, Sassoon's friends urged him to apply for a position as an instructor with the Officers' Training Corps at Cambridge. Sassoon was unwilling to do so. As Sassoon's friend, Lady Ottoline, later reported, "How could he possibly train others to go out there knowing what they would have to go through. 'They will all be killed or maimed.'"

In the final stanzas of "Conscripts," the reader senses a shift in attitude on the part of the narrator. Initially scornful of the recruits' lack of discipline and naïve ignorance, he gradually reveals how connected he has come to feel to these men, finally asserting that not only did the least attractive of these conscripts reveal "stubborn-hearted virtues," but "in extremis," came through with flying colors and "stood and played the hero to the end."

Here "Conscripts" offers an interesting glance into the class-distinctions within the army. In the early stages of the war, before heavy losses made it easier for soldiers to rise through the ranks, officers were picked from the privileged classes, of which Sassoon himself was a member. The theme of class awareness reappears in several of his poems, including "The March-Past," "In the Pink," "Base Details," and "The General." In "Conscripts," the common men display pure, hopeful, simple virtues, while the elites are presented as effeminate and unable to cope with the war's toughness and danger. Thus, as Sassoon bitterly writes, while the good men paid with their life for doing their duty, "many a sickly, slender lord who'd filled / My soul long since with lutanies of sin, / Went home, because they couldn't stand the din."

"Conscripts" has been cited for revealing the relationship between Sassoon's latent homosexual feelings and his help and care for his men. In a 1911 letter to Edward Carpenter, who was then among the leading English experts on homosexuality, Sassoon wrote about coming to terms with his own homosexuality:

> Until I read the "Intermediate Sex" [Carpenter's book], I knew absolutely nothing of that subject . . . & what ideas I had about homosexuality were absolutely prejudiced, & I was in such a groove that I couldn't allow myself to be what I wished to be, & the intense

attraction I felt for my own sex was almost a subconscious thing, &
my antipathy for women a mystery to me. . . .

Sassoon's homosexuality is never openly expressed in the war
poems, although in his diary he did admit to being in love with
fellow lieutenant David Thomas. Some critics have argued that the
intense compassion Sassoon felt for his men was at least in part a
result of his sublimation of any homosexual feelings, which were
socially taboo.

Regardless of how central a role his homosexuality played,
Sassoon's outrage and remorse reemerges again and again in his
poetry. ❀

Critical Views on
"Conscripts"

[Patrick Campbell's work includes *Wordsworth and Coleridge Lyrical Ballads: Critical Perspectives* (1991) and *Siegfried Sassoon: A Study of the War Poetry* (1999). In this excerpt, Campbell gives a close reading of Sassoon's "Conscripts," arguing that its examination of the tension between public and private identities marks it as a watershed poem.]

In "Conscripts," Sassoon forsakes the short epigrammatic sally, which had become his stock-in-trade during convalescence in England, for a longer reflective piece—five stanzas of six lines with rhymed couplets at the end of each verse—in which the irony, for once, is directed at himself. Shortly to return to France and the trenches (his trip from Southampton to Le Havre on 15 February occasioned the diary poem "Life-Belts"), "Conscripts" takes as subject Sassoon's drilling of young men at Litherland, an activity which he had recorded in his diary of 27 December, 1916: "Clumsy recruits . . . *On* garrrd! Long-point at the stomach etc. Red-and-black-striped-jersey instructors with well-poised bodies and wasp-waists, moving easily among the bunchy, awkward privates—pathetic crowd of willy-nilly patriots and (?) heroes!" The question-mark provides an important clue to the poem's summational stance: initially scornful of recruits' "attractive attitudes" that have no place on the parade-ground, the speaker gradually reveals how unwillingly he accepts his role of squad bully, and final answers his own journal query about "heroes" by asserting that in the finally analysis not only did the least attractive of these "squaddies" reveal "stubborn-hearted virtues," but, "in extremis," came through with flying colors—"stood and played the hero to the end."

The poem is, "inter alia," a manifestation of Sassoon's attempt to express his personal feelings in a way acceptable to his readership. True, it begins as a public poem on an innocuous theme, the drilling of raw recruits (*c.f.* Henry Reed's Second World War poem, "Naming of Parts"), a piece that could be published in *The Spectator* without causing offense. Indeed, writing to Lady Ottoline Morrell, Sassoon alerted her to its impending appearance in print, adding, "So I am really becoming highly respectable."

But the middle section reveals the suppressed emotions of the parade-ground; the enforced role of "raucous" martinet contrasts not only with Sassoon's romantic and libertarian spirit—"how I longed to set them free"—but with homoerotic longings barely concealed by the employment of such arch personifications as "Young Fancy—how I loved him all the while," the parapraxis of "joy was slack" and the innuendo of the drill command to "Press on your butts!" Indeed the final "confession" hints at a sexual activity which, while it may be more desired than actualized, is not altogether erased by the deliberately flippant tone of:

> And many a sickly, slender lord who'd filled
> My soul long since with lutanies of sin,
> Went home, because they couldn't stand the din.

The passage provoked an extraordinary reaction from Sassoon's friend Edmund Gosse. To Morrell the poet revealed: "Gosse wrote and rebuked me for my 'libel on the House of Lords' in the *Spectator* one. I can't imagine how he read such a thing into the harmless lines."

The transition from lust to war is significant, both in the context of these "harmless lines" and in terms of Sassoon's progress as a war poet. Honest enough to confront his feelings, however obliquely in the poem, Sassoon characteristically assuages his sense of personal guilt about his sexuality by declaring his faith in the common soldier's virtues. The poem's gnomic conclusion offers an encomium to "kind, common men"; it is the "awkward squad" of the opening line rather than "sickly slender" aristocrats who will not only stubbornly endure, but who will be metamorphosed, finally, into be-ribboned heroes. It is the *poet*, both as clandestine lover of men of his own class and as public parade-ground bully, who needs to reproach himself; he has feelings for some of these conscripts but will still be prepared to ship "them all to France" and possible death. Ironically and disturbingly, it is those he "despised" on the parade-ground, those he can "count as friend" "hardly a man of them" because of their ordinariness, who will emerge as heroes. Now free of any erotic or elitist prejudice imposed on them by the voyeuristic poet, they will not only survive the war but will march "resplendent home with crowns and stars."

—Patrick Campbell, *Siegfried Sassoon: A Study of the War Poetry* (Jefferson, N.C.: McFarland, 1999): pp. 136–37.

Arthur E. Lane on Realism in Sassoon's War Poems

[In this excerpt, Lane considers Sassoon's poem "Conscripts" in light of his growing reliance on a realist approach to narrating his wartime experiences. Lane is the author of *An Adequate Response: The War Poetry of Wilfred Owen and Siegfried Sassoon* (1972).]

Sassoon's wartime change to what he calls "realism" in poetry is the subject of the poem "Conscripts." His pastoral romanticism, dependent on an idea of what poetry ought to be, rather than on observed reality, fails him when he is confronted with a world which has not evolved in the modes of pastoral prettiness. "Conscripts" allegorizes his stock of poetic responses in terms of military reality; these are stanzas 1 and 4:

> "Fall in, that awkward squad, and strike no more
> Attractive attitudes! Dress by the right!
> The luminous rich colours that you wore
> Have changed to hueless khaki in the night.
> Magic? What's magic got to do with you?
> There's no such thing! Blood's red, and skies are blue."
>
> . . . .
>
> Their training done, I shipped them all to France,
> Where most of those I'd loved too well got killed.
> Rapture and pale Enchantment and Romance,
> And many a sickly, slender lord who'd filled
> My soul long since with lutanies of sin,
> Went home, because they couldn't stand the din.

Incidentally, the poem may itself provide an example of the dangers of poetic abstraction—or at least the dangers of not knowing when a poem is using figurative imagery. Perhaps remembering the embarrassments of the nineties, Sir Edmund Gosse objected strenuously to the fourth stanza of "Conscripts," particularly to its last three lines. Robert Graves, maintaining a straight face, records that Gosse considered that the lines "might be read as a libel on the British House of Lords. The peerage, he said, was proving itself splendidly heroic in the war."

By November 1915, Sassoon had completed his training as an infantry officer at Litherland, near Liverpool, and was sent to the western front. As "Conscripts" and Robert Graves indicate, he took his myths with him; but he lost them swiftly, and set about to disabuse an audience which was eventually to include Winston Churchill. Whether Churchill was disabused—or could have been disabused—is a moot point; when he talked to Sassoon in 1918, his intention seems to have been that of enlightening the younger man:

> Pacing the room, with a big cigar in the corner of his mouth, he gave me an emphatic vindication of militarism as an instrument of policy and stimulator of glorious individual achievements, not only in the mechanism of warfare but in spheres of social progress. The present war, he asserted, had brought about inventive discoveries which would ameliorate the condition of mankind. For example, there had been immense improvements in sanitation. Transfixed and submissive in my chair, I realized that what had begun as a persuasive confutation of my anti-war conviction was now addressed, in pauseful and perorating prose, to no one in particular.

Sassoon, understandably enough, avoided debate. Like Owen, he had come to realize that there were no easy solutions to the vexing problem of a war in progress. "Had I been capable of disputing with him," he concludes. "I might have well quoted four lines from *The Dynasts*:

> I have beheld the agonies of war
> Through many a weary season; seen enough
> To make me hold that scarcely any goal
> Is worth the reaching by so red a road."

"Conscripts" is a convenient poetic marker. From this point on, Sassoon's own initiation into "the agonies of war," his poems will fall into two main categories: war poems of dramatic realism like "The Hero" and the more purely satirical war poems like "Base Details."

—Arthur E. Lane, *An Adequate Response: The War Poetry of Wilfred Owen and Siegfried Sassoon* (Detroit: Wayne State University Press, 1972): pp. 93–95.

[George Parfitt is a literary scholar and editor whose works include *John Dryden: Selected Criticism* (editor with James Kinsley) (1970), *Ben Jonson: The Complete Poems,* (1975), *Fiction of the First World War* (1987), and *English Poetry of the First World War* (1988). He has also served as editor of *Renaissance and Modern Studies.* In this selection from *English Poetry of the First World War,* Parfitt analyzes Sassoon's use of satire in his poetic responses to the war.]

Siegfried Sassoon is remembered as *the* satirical poet of the war, and of the war's better-known poets he is the one who is most consistently satirical of aspects of war experience. But several points need to be made about Sassoon's satire, and how this came to be his dominant mode.

Sassoon was not a satirist before the war. The version of self he fictionalises as the pre-war George Sherston is essentially one of ignorance and philistinism: and this exercise in fictional autobiography can be seen as nostalgic satire, with Sherston's immersion in the war reflecting on his Edwardian innocence. ⟨. . .⟩

But if Sassoon did not go to war as a satirist, he quickly became one. 'Absolution,' of April–September 1915, is Brookean, with its themes of absolution, the shining out of beauty and the war as a scourge which brings wisdom and freedom, but Sassoon's own retrospective note pins the poem down as a typical early response: 'People used to feel like this when they "joined up" in 1914 and 1915. No one feels it when they "go out again."' His dates suggest that people who 'went out again' quickly began to feel the confusion, exhaustion and pressure which he catches in 'The Redeemer,' but that poem is not satirical, and several others follow before 'In the Pink,' of February 1916. Sassoon says that the *Westminster Review* rejected this latter poem 'as they thought it might prejudice recruiting!!'. The Davies of the poem is ignorant and doomed:

> To-night he's in the pink; but soon he'll die.
> And still the war goes on—he don't know why.

But this weariness and lack of known purpose constitute potential rather than actual satire.

Poems seem to have come in rapid succession for Sassoon in 1916, and they quickly begin to show revision of the values and ideals of the war's beginning. There is observation of the unpleasant—'the brown rats, the nimble scavengers' of 'Golgotha'—and the sardonic contrast in 'A Subaltern' between earlier summer days (with a parody of Newbolt—'twenty runs to make, and last man in') and the rats, slime and 'palsied weather' of this 'Hell.' The writing comes close to satire at times:

> O Jesus, send me a wound to-day
> And I'll believe in Your bread and wine,
> And get my bloody old sins washed white!
>   ('Stand-to: Good Friday Morning')

There is identification with the enemy ('A Night Attack'); the sardonic acceptance of amputation as a release from the fighting ('The One-Legged Man'); and, in 'The Death-Bed,' a moment when the poet begins to set his satirical sights:

> He's young; he hated War; how should he die
> When cruel old campaigners win safe through?

Sassoon notes that this poem was 'Refused by the *Westminster* without comment.'

A common theme of Adcock's *For Remembrance* is that the young men of his account did not like war, and this can be linked with the idea that Britain was anxious to avoid conflict. War is forced upon the nation, but is made acceptable because the cause is good and war can be a cleansing. Sassoon's poems, however, move to satire as he registers no cleansing and the physical and psychological cost which is being exacted. The satire comes out of the experiential pressure which is its validification; and it comes to seem the inevitable result of that pressure. Two or three preliminary points should be made. The first is that the detail of the accounts of trench experience provides the justification for satire (which is not to say that the targets of his satire are necessarily and always the most appropriate ones); the second, that Sassoon does not satirise the military enemy (who, where treated, are seen as suffering in the same situation); the third, that Sassoon's poems do not satirise either ranker or subaltern.

—George Parfitt, *English Poetry of the First World War: Contexts and Themes* (New York: Harvester Wheatsheaf, 1990): pp. 42, 43–44.

Thematic Analysis of
"Attack"

"Attack" was one of two trench-line poems written during October 1917 and published in the *Cambridge Magazine* of that same year. The poem was later included among the 39 poems in Sassoon's collection of poetry, *Counter-Attack*. Sassoon composed "Attack" after witnessing the Hindenburg Line attack, which capped off a particularly grueling period of the war. In the midst of the attack, Sassoon wrote in his diary, "The dead bodies . . . are beyond description especially after the rain. . . . Our shelling of the line—and subsequent bombing etc.—has left a number of mangled Germans; they will haunt me till I die."

The poem's central focus is that most desperate of all battle procedures: "going over the top," that moment when "time ticks bland and busy on their wrists." In "Attack," the landscape itself seems to be conspiring against the men. The dawn, which should bring the hopeful promise of a new day, here merely brings the men that much closer to possible death, with the sun "smouldering" through smoke that hides the "menacing scarred slope." The movement of the men themselves is awkward and almost clownish; the tanks "creep and topple forward" and the men are "clumsily bowed."

Everything about the men's physical description—from their hesitant, lurching movements to their fearful and furtive countenances—is at odds with the usual heroic ideals of the time. Here the soldiers wait, animal-like, for an almost certain death. Surrounded by all the trappings of war—tanks, bombs, guns, shovels, battle-gear, even wristwatches—the men are nonetheless vulnerable, exposed, and utterly alone when they go over the top.

Sassoon's emphasis on the details of a particular situation allows him, as one critic observed, "to build up the outcry of the human being under extreme pressure." Until the last two lines, the reader's perspective of the activity in the poem is distanced and unspecific. Only as the men stumble and flounder and climb their way out of the trenches does a single human voice emerge, personifying the fear and desperation of going over the top. His cry—"O Jesus, make it stop!"—renders the emotional intensity of combat that much more excruciating, from the agony of waiting to the desperate hurling forward of the soldiers' own bodies, most likely to their death.

In "Attack," as in some of his other poems, Sassoon almost didactically insists on the facts and details of war as an attempt to force public acceptance of the stark realities of trench warfare. Sassoon often self-consciously drew on the work of Thomas Hardy, a poet whose evocation of the darker side of life caused him to be dismissed as a pessimist; Hardy's artistic credo from "In Tenebris, II" was "if way to the Better there be, it exacts a full look at the Worst." The importance Sassoon himself placed on realism is revealed in his 1939 lecture entitled "On Poetry," in which he argues for simple, direct communication in poetry. Abstraction, expressionism, and other hallmarks of modernist poetry, Sassoon says, make poetry unintelligible and therefore irrelevant. The poet, according to Sassoon, should speak directly and convey his or her feelings to a reader made sympathetic by the language itself. By resorting to the simplest and most honest language, he continued, "the utterance may be magnificent, or it may be un-emphatic; but there is never any doubt about its directness and humanity. I mean the true vocal cadence of something urgently communicated—the best words in the best order—yes—but empowered also by sincerity and inspiration."

Sassoon, of course, was not the only poet of the time who felt that the war necessitated a new, more effective idiom. As D. H. Lawrence observed in 1916:

> The essence of poetry with us in this age of stark and unlovely actualities is a stark directness, without a shadow of a life, or a shadow of deflection anywhere. Everything can go, but this stark, bare, rocky directness of statement, this alone makes poetry, to-day.

In his dogged and unswerving determination to make what he had witnessed and experienced at the Front intelligible to the uninitiated reader, Sassoon created an unvarnished, almost documentary record of the war. Critics have since argued that in doing so Sassoon sacrificed the complexity of his feelings about the war in a single-minded campaign to valorize the common soldier as he attacked the noncombatant population. ❈

Critical Views on
"Attack"

[Patrick Campbell is the author of *Siegfried Sassoon: A Study of the War Poetry*. In this selection from the book, Campbell examines how Sassoon considered his war poems—the poems for which he would be remembered— as his least important writing.]

⟨. . .⟩ As though in illustration of the truism that artists are notoriously bad judges of their own work, Sassoon later recorded his regret that he was still lionized as a trench poet when he wanted to be remembered as a devotional poet first and foremost, and as a prose memoirist second. In a letter to the critic Michael Thorpe in 1966, the now reclusive poet emphasized this personal hierarchy of value, declaring, "I am a firm believer in the Memoirs; and am inclined to think that the war poems (the significant and successful ones) will end up as mere appendices to the matured humanity of the Memoirs."

In the same letter Sassoon consigned his war poems, if not to oblivion, then at least to the bottom of his filing cabinet. Not only were they, in his estimation, inferior to his mature work, they frequently got in the way of readers' proper appreciation of it. "My renown as a War Poet," he declared, "has now become a positive burden to me, which makes your kind recognition of the later poems specially valuable to me." Moreover, Sassoon was at pains to remind his correspondent that the verses of *Counter-Attack* (1918), and to a lesser extent those of *The Old Huntsman* (1917) and *Picture-Show* (1919), had been dashed off by a headstrong young officer too caught up by events to view them dispassionately. His artistic success, now almost half a century back, was still cause for astonishment: "I was immature, impulsive, irrational and bewildered by the whole affair, hastily improvising my responses and only saved by being true to the experiences which I drew upon." But that last observation was of course the nub of the matter. It was precisely Sassoon's insistence on the truth, his desire to tell it how it was or at least how it felt at the time, that endeared him both to increasing numbers of his fellow soldiers and to a discerning public at home.

Sassoon's considered judgment on his early progress as a poet was equally sweeping, not to say disingenuous. Characterizing his development in terms of schoolboyish clichés, he maintained:

> I was never a professional writer and in some ways a complete amateur. In 1919 I was still in "the Lower Fifth" and the next six years were spent in trying to get into "the Upper Sixth." *Satirical Poems* (published in 1926) was an exercise in learning to use words with accuracy (the content was only playing a mental game without deep seriousness) and those years were a process of getting the war out of my system. . . . I did not find my real voice until 1924. . . .

Allowing for the fact that the whole notion of professionalism was abhorrent to Sassoon—witness his patrician perspective on fox-hunting, race-riding, golfing and cricketing—and for his recurrent wish to leap back to a pre-war Edwardian idyll, it is nonetheless extraordinary that he should disparage the trench poetry as "Lower Fifth" versifying. It is a critical commonplace that *Satirical Poems* (1926) are, to use Sassoon's own words, "exercises," occasional verses often composed without any compelling sense of occasion, misnomers in that they precisely lack that intensity which typified the "Blighty" satires or, for that matter, the bulletins from the battlefield. His contention that he did not discover his "real" poetic voice until 1924 is not shared by admirers of the war poetry.

Posterity has, furthermore, failed to uphold Sassoon's wish to be remembered as a significant devotional poet. At the end of his life no one knew that reluctant truth better than the poet. In *Letters to a Critic,* he bemoaned the fact that "most reviewers have shied away (the equine metaphor is instructive) from my spiritual pilgrimage." Where critics had responded, they offered not only "heart-breaking" reviews of *Sequences* (sixteen years in gestation), but a crippling denial of the poet's spirituality. Only Blunden, he recollected, "asserted that I am essentially a religious poet."

No one today, encountering Sassoon's *Collected Poems,* would deny this assertion: his spiritual pilgrimage, begun in the twenties and haltingly presaged in such war verses as "A Mystic as Soldier," slowly gathered momentum and culminated in his being received into the Roman Catholic Church in 1957. In terms of sheer quantity, the religious poetry bulks large. But it pales in comparison with the blood and thunder of verses imbued with fierce anger at Home Front hypocrisies, or with strenuous compassion for the suffering soldier. No spiritual experience, no matter how intensely felt, is likely to reach a significant readership unless it is couched in vividly realized imagery; on the battlefield the all too tangible events and experiences were a quarry of memorable images waiting to be encapsulated in verse.

—Patrick Campbell, Siegfried Sassoon: A Study of the War Poetry
(Jefferson, North Carolina: McFarland, 1999): pp. 2–4.

JOHN H. JOHNSTON ON THE FELLOWSHIP OF SUFFERING IN THE WAR POEMS

[John Johnston is Professor of English at West Virginia University, Morgantown, and the author of *English Poetry of the First World War: A Study in the Evolution of Lyric and Narrative Form* (1964) and a contributor to the *Encyclopedia of World Literature in the Twentieth Century* and to the *Review of Politics*. In this section, Johnston discusses Sassoon's tendency to overwhelm the reader with graphic depictions of the war as a way of conveying the intense emotional reaction he felt. In doing so, Johnston argues, Sassoon was often in danger of creating a confused and ultimately distorted vision of the war.]

Other poems in *Counter-Attack* both portray and embody the emotional intensities of combat. "Attack," for instance, depicts the terrible anxiety of men about to cross the parapets:

> Lines of grey, muttering faces, masked with fear,
> They leave their trenches, going over the top,
> While time ticks blank and busy on their wrists,
> And hope, with furtive eyes and grappling fists,
> Flounders in mud. O Jesus, make it stop!

The fellowship of suffering completes Sassoon's identification with the men he must lead "To the foul beast of war that bludgeons life."

Unlike Owen, he describes the demoralizing psychological effects of battle more often than wounds or physical anguish, and for the first time poetry reveals what modern scientific violence can do to men's minds. Sassoon's soldiers are numb with fear or horror, or they break down completely under the prolonged emotional strain of trench fighting. He pays tribute, of course, to the courage and tenacity of his "brave brown companions," but he never makes that bravery the subject of a specific poem. If young Hughes, in "Wirers," exerts himself manfully in repairing the barbed-wire defences in No Man's Land, Sassoon gives the account a bitter twist that nullifies any heroism involved:

> Young Hughes was badly hit; I heard him carried away,
> Moaning at every lurch; no doubt he'll die to-day.
> But *we* can say the front-line wire's been safely mended.

One wonders how much positive action and achievement is excluded from *Counter-Attack* in the interest of thematic unity. As an anti-war propagandist, Sassoon could hardly depict a successful attack or even an incident representing individual heroism; he could hardly portray a soldier mastering his own emotional turmoil and responding to the imperatives of duty. To write about such things would have been to grant that the war had some positive moral or historical significance, and Sassoon was in no state of mind to make such an admission. ⟨. . .⟩

—John H. Johnston, *English Poetry of the First World War: A Study in the Evolution of Lyric and Narrative Form* (Princeton, New Jersey: Princeton University Press, 1964): pp. 101–2.

THOMAS MALLON ON SASSOON'S MEMORY OF THE WAR

[Thomas Mallon contributed to *Modernism Reconsidered*, which was edited by Robert Kiely and John Hildebidle. In this chapter, Mallon adds insights to the experiences behind Sassoon's war memories.]

The stage nerves Seigfried Sassoon may have experienced before addressing the Poetry Club at the Harvard Union in the spring of

1920 were mitigated by the formidable assurances of Miss Amy Lowell, who had recently written to tell him that he "was the one man whom the Harvard undergraduates wanted to hear." Such assurances were more necessary than might be supposed; Sassoon had discovered upon arriving in New York in January that, little more than a year after the Armistice, more than enough British authors were touring America to fill the already slackening desire to hear from and about the soldier-poets. In fact, the war was sufficiently receding in people's minds that Sassoon had to rely on himself, rather than the Pond Lyceum Bureau, to scare up most of his engagements. But at Harvard Sassoon did find a receptive audience for the last of his pleas against militarism, and he finished his tour feeling that his "diminutive attempt to make known to Americans an interpretation of the war as seen by the fighting men" had been "not altogether ineffective."

In some respects the Harvard appearance was the end of a phase in Sassoon's life that began in 1917 with the appearance of *The Old Huntsman* and his public statement against the war, climaxed with the publication of *Counter-Attack* on June 27, 1918, and had its denouement in his post-Armistice lecture tour. In less than four years he went from being a sometime versifier to something of an international literary celebrity, the man who more than any other had brought about the post-Somme poetic rebellion in diction, subject matter, and outlook. Without question these were the most public years of his life, and although he would live for nearly another half century, nothing in his later works would so impress itself on readers' minds and literary history as the angry ironies of "Base Details," "The General," "To Any Dead Officer," and "Suicide in the Trenches." ⟨. . .⟩

Sassoon says that the self which stood in a sunny Trafalgar Square one day after his arrival from America "realized that he had come to the end of the journey on which he had set out when he enlisted in the army six years before. And, though he wasn't clearly conscious of it, time has since proved that there was nothing for him to do but begin all over again." But if he did begin again, it was mostly to explore his "impercipient past," first in the Sherston books which were, he admits, in some ways a substitute for the long poem Gosse urged him to write, and then in the actual autobiographies. Certainly nothing to equal the literary impact of *Counter-Attack* was again to come from his pen. He was eventually to become Heytesbury's hermit. In a sense he went home from that Saturday afternoon in Trafalgar Square more to recall life than to live it; his uncertain efforts toward existence were over and a sort of afterlife had begun.

In the final pages of *Siegfried's Journey,* Sassoon speculates:

> Once in his lifetime, perhaps, a man may be the instrument through which something constructive emerged, whether it be genius giving birth to an original idea or the anonymous mortal who makes the most of an opportunity which will never recur. It is for the anonymous ones that I have my special feeling. I like to think of them remembering the one time when they were involved in something unusual or important—when, probably without knowing it at the time, they, as it were, wrote their single masterpiece, never to perform anything comparable again. Then they were fully alive, living above themselves, and discovering powers they hadn't been aware of. For a moment they stood in the transfiguring light of dramatic experience. And nothing ever happened to them afterwards. They were submerged by human uneventfulness. It is only since I got into my late fifties that I have realized these great tracts of insignificance in people's lives. My younger self scornfully rejected the phrase "getting through life" as reprehensible. That I now accept it with an equanimity which amounts almost to affection is my way of indicating the contrast between our states of mind. The idea of oblivion attracts me; I want, after life's fitful fever, to sleep well.

Surely the remarks on "anonymous ones" apply to no one more than himself, however much shielding is given by the third person and the plural; and even the distance between the older and younger selves he contrasts is not as great as he imagines it to be. Sassoon says that the younger one "scornfully rejected the phrase 'getting through life'"; yet the essential passivity of that self is more to be remarked on than anything else. The older autobiographer is just giving final intellectual acceptance to what, for all its fitful rebellions and genuine heroism, was the essential temper and practice of his youth. The later perspective is neither so long, nor the sensibility so different, as the older Sassoon thinks. The narrative lacunae, present-tense reveries, and watercolored judgments found in the autobiographies all spring from the mental and emotional habits of his younger days. Not only is the child father to the man, in this case; the sporadic boy-poet is father to the autobiographer.

Sassoon writes that he is "inclined to compare the living present to a jig-saw puzzle loose in its box. Not until afterwards can we fit the pieces together and make a coherent picture of them. While writing this book I have often been conscious of this process." But that process does not go very far toward coherence. Just when Sassoon wonders if it can be "that the immediacy of our existence amounts to little more than animality, and that our ordered understanding of it is only assembled through afterthought and retrospection," he stops short: "But I am overstraining my limited intelligence and must extricate myself from these abstrusities."

Although both sets of recollections are full of amused self-depreciation, this last line comes not from coyness or false modesty. Sassoon's interpretive intelligence was and remained limited. It could not be otherwise. The dreaming and tentative boy was not meant to become a thinker at thirty-four or even fifty-nine. To say that this is a limitation in his character is to say very little, because it is also the key to that character's unusual beauty. There was something permanently inviolate about it, even in the most exciting and dangerous circumstances. And much of it survived the "old century" well into the miseries of the mid-twentieth. Sassoon remained in large part unreachable to life.

It took a higher power to break the spell. God came to him late, but succeeded in transporting him fully and finally. Religion brought his last volumes of verse new life, and he awaited the next world with far more sustained ambition and interest than he ever really displayed toward this one. But this is another, and better, story.

—Thomas Mallon, "The Great War and Sassoon's Memory," *Modernism Reconsidered*, ed. Robert Kiely and John Hildebidle (Cambridge, Massachusetts: Harvard University Press, 1983): pp. 81–82, 97–99.

Works by the
Poets of World War I

Rupert Brooke

Poems. 1911.

1914 and Other Poems. 1915.

Lithuania. 1915.

John Webster and the Elizabethan Drama. 1916.

Letters from America. 1916.

The Collected Poems of Rupert Brooke. 1918.

The Poetical Works of Rupert Brooke, ed. Geoffrey Keynes. 1946.

Democracy and the Arts. 1946.

The Prose of Rupert Brooke, ed. Christopher Hassall. 1956.

The Letters of Rupert Brooke, ed. Geoffrey Keynes. 1968.

Rupert Brooke: a Reappraisal and Selection, ed. Timothy Rogers. 1971.

Letters from Rupert Brooke to His Publisher, 1911–1914. 1975.

*Rupert Brooke and James Strachey: The Hidden Correspondence,
1905–1915,* ed. Keith Hale. 1998.

Siegfried Sassoon

Poems. 1906.

Orpheus in Diloeryium. 1908.

Sonnets. 1909.

Sonnets and Verses. 1909.

Twelve Sonnets. 1911.

Poems. 1911.

An Ode for Music. 1912.

Hyacinth: An Idyll. 1912

Melodies. 1912.

The Daffodil Murderer. 1913 (written under pseudonym Saul Kain).

Discoveries. 1915.

Morning Glory. 1916.

The Old Huntsman and Other Poems. 1918.

Counter-Attack and Other Poems. 1918.

The War Poems of Siegfried Sassoon. 1919.

Picture-Show. 1919.

Recreations. 1923.

Lingual Exercises for Advanced Vocabularians. 1925.

Selected Poems. 1925.

Satirical Poems. 1926.

The Heart's Journey. 1927.

Poems by Pinchebeck Lyre. 1931.

The Road to Ruin. 1933.

Vigils. 1934.

The Old Century and Seven More Years. 1938.

Rhymed Ruminations. 1939.

Poems Newly Selected 1916–1935. 1940.

The Complete Memoirs of George Sherston. 1940.

The Weald of Youth (autobiography). 1942.

Siegfried's Journey: 1916–1920 (autobiography). 1946.

Meredith, a Biography. 1948.

Letters to a Critic. 1976.

Diaries 1920–1922. 1981.

Diaries 1915–1918. 1983.

Siegfried Sassoon Letters to Max Beerbohm. 1986.

Works About
World War I Poets

Abercrombie, Lascelles. *The Idea of Great Poetry*. London: M. Secker, 1925.

Bergonzi, Bernard. *Heroes' Twilight: A Study of the Literature of the Great War*. London: Constable, 1965.

Bewley, Marius. *Masks & Mirrors: Essays in Criticism*. New York: Atheneum, 1970.

Caesar, Adrian. *Taking It Like a Man: Suffering, Sexuality and the War Poets: Brooke, Sassoon, Owen, Graves*. New York: Manchester University Press, 1993.

Cohen, Joseph. *Journey to the Trenches: The Life of Isaac Rosenberg 1890–1918*. London: Robson Books, 1975.

———. "The Three Roles of Siegfried Sassoon." *Tulane Studies in English* 7 (1957): 169–85.

———. "The War Poet as Archetypal Spokesman." *Stand* 4, no. 3 (1960): 23–27.

———. "Owen Agonistes." *English Literature in Transition* 8, no. 5 (December, 1965): 253–68.

Corrigan, Dame Felicitas. *Siegfried Sassoon: Poet's Pilgrimage*. London: Gollancz, 1973.

Daiches, David. "The Poetry of Wilfred Owen." In *New Literary Values: Studies in Modern Literature*. Edinburgh: Oliver and Boyd, 1936.

———. *Poetry and the Modern World*. Chicago: University of Chicago Press, 1940.

———. "Isaac Rosenberg: Poet." *Commentary* 10, no. 1 (July 1950): 91–3.

Davidson, Mildred. *The Poetry Is in the Pity*. London: Chatto & Windus, 1972.

Day Lewis, Cecil. *A Hope for Poetry*. Oxford: Basil Blackwell, 1934.

Delany, Paul. *The Neo-Pagans: Friendship and Love in the Rupert Brooke Circle*. London: Macmillan, 1987.

Durrell, Lawrence. *A Key to Modern British Poetry*. Norman: University of Oklahoma Press, 1952.

Fussell, Paul. *The Great War and Modern Memory*. Oxford: Oxford University Press, 1975.

Harding, D. W. *Experience into Words.* New York: Horizon Press, 1964.

Gardner, Brian. *Up the Line to Death: The War Poets 1914–1918: An Anthology.* London: Eyre Methuen, 1964.

Giddings, Robert. *The War Poets.* New York: Orion Books, 1988.

Gose, Elliott B., Jr. "Diggin In: An Interpretation of Wilfred Owen's 'Strange Meeting.'" In *College English* 22 (March, 1961).

Graham, Desmond. *The Truth of War: Owen, Blunden, Rosenberg.* Manchester: Carcanet Press, 1984

Graves, Robert. *Good-bye to All That.* New York: Doubleday Anchor Books, 1957.

Hassall, Christopher. *Rupert Brooke.* New York: Harcourt, Brace & World, 1964.

Hibberd, Dominic. *Wilfred Owen: The Last Year 1917–1918.* London: Constable and Company, 1992.

Hughes, Ted. "The Crime of Fools Exposed." *New York Times Books* (12 April 1964): 4, 18.

Johnston, John H. *English Poetry of the First World War: A Study in the Evolution of Lyric and Narrative Form.* Princeton, New Jersey: Princeton University Press, 1964.

Lane, Arthur E. *An Adequate Response: The War Poetry of Wilfred Owen and Siegfried Sassoon.* Detroit, Michigan: Wayne State University Press, 1972.

Larkin. Philip. "The War Poet." *The Listener* (10 October 1963): 561–62.

Lehmann, John. *The Strange Destiny of Rupert Brooke.* New York: Holt, Rinehart and Winston, 1980.

Mallon, Thomas. "The Great War and Sassoon's Memory," in *Modernism Reconsidered.* ed. Robert Kiely and John Hildebidle. Cambridge: Harvard University Press, 1983.

Moeyes, Paul. *Siegfried Sassoon: Scorched Glory.* London: Macmillan, 1997.

Murry, John Middleton. *The Evolution of an Intellectual.* London: Richard Cobden-Sanderson, 1920.

Parfitt, George. *English Poetry of the First World War: Contexts and Themes.* New York: Harvester Wheatsheaf, 1990.

Parsons, I. M. "The Poems of Wilfred Owen (1893–1918)." *New Criterion* 10. (July 1931): 658–69.

Pearsall, Robert Brainard. *Rupert Brooke: The Man and Poet.* Amsterdam: Editions Rodopi, 1974.

Purkis, John. *A Preface to Wilfred Owen.* New York: Addison Wesley Longman, 1999.

Quinn, Patrick J. *The Great War and the Missing Muse: The Early Writings of Robert Graves and Siegfried Sassoon.* London: Associated University Press, 1994.

Roberts, Beth Ellen. *The Female God of Isaac Rosenberg: A Muse for Wartime. English Literature in Transition 1880–1920* 39, no. 3 (1996): 319–32.

Shelton, Carole. "War Protest, Heroism and Shellshock: Siegfried Sassoon: A Case Study." *Focus on Robert Graves* 1, no. 13 (winter 1992).

Silken, Jon. *Out of Battle: The Poetry of the Great War.* New York: St. Martin's, 1998.

———, editor. *The Penguin Book of First World War Poetry.* Second Edition. New York: Penguin Books, 1996.

Stallworthy, Jon. *Wilfred Owen.* London: Oxford University Press, 1974.

Thomas, Dylan. "Wilfred Owen." In *Quite Early One Morning.* London: J. M. Dent & Sons, 1954.

Thorpe, Michael. *Siegfried Sassoon: A Critical Study.* Leiden, Netherlands: Universitaire Pers, 1966.

Van Doren, Mark. "War and Peace." *The Nation* (25 May 1921): 747.

Welland, D. S. R. *Wilfred Owen: A Critical Study.* London: Chatto & Windus, 1960.

Wilson, Jean Moorcroft. *Siegfried Sassoon: The Making of a War Poet, a Biography (1896–1918).* New York: Routledge, 1999.

Winter, Jay. *Sites of Memory, Sites of Mourning: The Great War in European Cultural History.* Cambridge, England: Cambridge University Press, 1995.

Wohl, Robert. *The Generation of 1914.* Cambridge, Massachusetts: Harvard University Press, 1979.

Yeats, W. B., editor. *The Oxford Book of Modern Verse.* New York: Oxford University Press, 1936.

Acknowledgments

Rupert Brooke: A Reappraisal and Selection from His Writings, Some Hitherto Unpublished by Timothy Rogers (London: Routledge and Kegan Paul, 1971). © 1971 by Routledge. Reprinted by permission.

Rupert Brooke: His Life and His Legend by John Lehmann (London: Weidenfeld and Nicolson, 1980). © 1980 by Weidenfeld and Nicolson. Reprinted by permission.

Heroes' Twilight: A Study of the Literature of the Great War by Bernard Bergonzi (London: Constable and Company, 1965). © 1965 by Constable and Company. Reprinted by permission of Carcanet Press Ltd.

Rupert Brooke by Christopher Hassall (New York: Harcourt, Brace and World, 1964). © 1964 by Faber and Faber. Reprinted by permission.

Rupert Brooke: The Man and Poet by Robert Brainard Pearsall (Amsterdam: Rodopi N.V., 1974). © 1974 by Rodopi. Reprinted by permission.

Review of *The Collected Poems of Rupert Brooke* by Virginia Woolf. From *The Times Literary Supplement* (8 August 1918). © 1918 by *The Times Literary Supplement*. Reprinted by permission.

"Death of Mr. Rupert Brooke" by Winston Churchill. From *The Times* (26 April 1915). © 1915 by *The Times*. Reprinted by permission.

Red Wine of Youth: A Life of Rupert Brooke by Arthur Stringer (New York: Bobbs-Merrill, 1948). © 1948 by Bobbs-Merrill. Reprinted by permission.

Out of Battle: The Poetry of the Great War, 2nd ed. by Jon Silkin (London: Macmillan, 1998). © 1998 by Jon Silkin. Reprinted by permission of Palgrave Macmillan.

Siegfried Sassoon: A Critical Study by Michael Thorpe (London: Oxford University Press, 1967). © 1967 by Oxford University Press. Reprinted by permission.

Index of
Themes and Ideas